WHAT TO DO
WHEN YOU
DON'T KNOW
WHAT TO DO

ALSO BY WYATT WEBB

It's Not about the Horse (with Cindy Pearlman)

✢❈✢

HAY HOUSE TITLES OF RELATED INTEREST

Books

An Attitude of Gratitude, by Keith D. Harrell
Being in Balance, by Dr. Wayne W. Dyer
Inner Peace for Busy People, by Joan Z. Borysenko, Ph.D.
Soul Coaching, by Denise Linn

Card Decks

Empowerment Cards, by Tavis Smiley
Self-Care Cards, by Cheryl Richardson
Wisdom Cards, by Louise L. Hay

✢❈✢

All of the above are available at your
local bookstore, or may be ordered by visiting:

Hay House USA: **www.hayhouse.com®**
Hay House Australia: **www.hayhouse.com.au**
Hay House UK: **www.hayhouse.co.uk**
Hay House South Africa: **www.hayhouse.co.za**
Hay House India: **www.hayhouse.co.in**

WHAT TO DO WHEN YOU DON'T KNOW WHAT TO DO

Common Horse Sense

WYATT WEBB

HAY HOUSE, INC.
Carlsbad, California • New York City
London • Sydney • Johannesburg
Vancouver • Hong Kong • New Delhi

Published and distributed in the United States by: Hay House, Inc.: www.
hayhouse.com • **Published and distributed in Australia by:** Hay House
Australia Pty. Ltd.: www.hayhouse.com.au • **Published and distributed
in the United Kingdom by:** Hay House UK, Ltd.: www.hayhouse.co.uk
• **Published and distributed in the Republic of South Africa by:** Hay
House SA (Pty), Ltd.: www.hayhouse.co.za • **Distributed in Canada
by:** Raincoast: www.raincoast.com • **Published in India by:** Hay House
Publishers India: www.hayhouse.co.in

Design: Tricia Breidenthal

(An adaptation of this book was previously issued in hardcover under the
title *Five Steps for Overcoming Fear and Self-Doubt:* Hay House, 2004)

Library of Congress Cataloging-in-Publication Data

Webb, Wyatt.
  What to do when you don't know what to do : common horse sense /
Wyatt Web.
    p. cm.
  ISBN-13: 978-1-4019-0790-7 (tradepaper)
  ISBN-10: 1-4019-0790-3 (tradepaper)
  1. Fear. 2. Self-doubt. 3. Self-confidence. 4. Spirituality. I. Title.
  BF575.F2W43 2006
  158.1--dc22

                              2005033870

ISBN 13: 978-1-4019-0790-7
ISBN 10: 1-4019-0790-3

13 12 11 10   6 5 4 3
1st printing, July 2006
3rd printing, March 2010

Printed in the United States of America

To Carin and Toby, fellow travelers.
Words cannot express the joy and
happiness you've brought to my life.
You are truly two of the bravest
souls I've ever known.

CONTENTS

PREFACE

Just when I thought I'd beaten the devil, I was proven wrong once again.

For as long as I can remember, I've always wanted to get away with something, but I've never been able to do so. On November 19, 2001, I was finally convinced of the universal law of cause and effect.

For those of us who live in Tucson, Arizona, it's not often that we look outside our windows and see a puddle of water. Tucson gets about 11 inches of rain per year, most of which falls during the six-week monsoon season in July and early August. On that November day, I looked outside and noticed standing water against the retaining wall in my front yard. Upon further investigation, I discovered that somewhere underneath, inside the plumbing system, there was quite a large leak.

I called a friend of mine who does a lot of the work around my home, and he came right over. He proceeded to dig up the wet area and quickly discovered a broken pipe in obvious need of repair. On that particular day he had a limited amount of time, so he repaired the broken pipe but had to leave before refilling the hole. I told him to go ahead; I'd take care of it myself.

I was almost finished filling in the hole and had gone around to the backyard to get the hose and wash down the sidewalk. Suddenly, it felt like the biggest elephant in Africa was standing in the middle of my chest. I'd never experienced pain like that before and immediately knew it had something to do with my heart.

My wife, Carin, came outside at that moment and saw me leaning against the wall. I told her that something was very wrong. She asked me to sit down, so I did. After a few minutes, I got up and went inside the house to lie down on the bed. Nothing seemed to help, so we called 911.

When the emergency-response crew didn't get there immediately, I began to get more frightened, so we jumped into the car and headed toward urgent care, meeting the ambulance on the way. At urgent care, the staff immediately put me on a gurney, rolled me into an examining room, and upon hearing my symptoms, gave me nitroglycerin. I realized that they don't give you that for sinus problems; thus, my suspicions about my heart were confirmed. They worked with me for quite some time before transferring me to the emergency room at a nearby hospital.

The fear that I experienced while lying on that gurney was unlike any that I'd ever known before, and I began to look at it closely. Although I had no idea how severe my condition was, I felt a calmness about what was going on. I'd said for some time that I had no fear of dying, and I realized at that point that it was true. (This had been the case a great deal of my life; most of my fears have been associated with living.) Yet, as I looked at Carin, I became aware of how much I wanted to stay on this planet and spend more time with her. I also realized that there were things I hadn't finished doing in my work, and I wanted to finish them. Most important, I knew I'd been put in touch with my mortality. I suddenly knew that it was possible for me to leave this life at any given moment, and it became clearer than ever that I had some choices to make about how I live my life.

Before I go any further, let me say a few words about my doctor. I'd been assigned one cardiologist, but a man with a different name showed up. When Dr. Gregory Koshkarian put his hand on my shoulder and looked into my eyes for the first time, I just knew I was going to be all right. The sound of his voice, the way he touched my shoulder, how he treated Carin—everything he did within those first few minutes—assured me that I was in excellent hands. I later found out that he was one of the premier cardiologists in Tucson and that he possessed superior technical skills, but in those first few minutes, none of that mattered. He appeared to have the soul of a healer, and I trusted him immediately.

I was admitted to the hospital and diagnosed with partial blockages in my arteries, which Dr. Koshkarian thought could be corrected with a routine angioplasty. I was scheduled to have the procedure the next day, and meanwhile, I was given morphine for the pain.

After a minute or two, I asked the nurse why I wasn't getting a head rush.

He looked at Carin and asked, "Is he an addict?"

"Yes," she said. "Recovering."

"Oh, that explains it," the nurse replied with a smile. Looking at me, he explained, "Mr. Webb, you don't get the rush when you use these drugs for their intended purpose, and that's to manage your pain."

Even in the midst of all the craziness, there was the opportunity for laughter.

Unfortunately, the laughter didn't last long. The next day, when Dr. Koshkarian got inside my heart, he found that the blockages were much more extensive and severe than he'd originally thought. I had 70, 80, and 90 percent blockages in five different places. He presented me with a choice: open-heart surgery or stainless steel stents to keep my arteries open and let the blood flow. I chose the stents.

Although I was awake for the entire procedure, I had no concept of how much time went by. The whole thing was supposed to take a couple of hours, but it turned out to require five hours and five stents. Dr. Koshkarian left the room a couple of times that I wasn't aware of and assured Carin that things were going well, proving once again that we were in the hands of the best physician and healer we could possibly be associated with. I stayed overnight in the hospital, was released the following day, and went back to work three days later.

During the first six months of my recovery time, I was hypersensitive to every little twinge that occurred. It seemed as if each little pain or skipped beat of the heart brought up fear for me. I realized that in order to deal with these particular fears, since I'd decided that I really wanted to be on this earth, I'd have to exercise what I'd been taught to do and was sharing with my clients in my work. The good news is that I had the tools at my disposal—I knew the five steps for overcoming fear and self-doubt—so once again, as I've done many times in my life, I applied them to this particular situation.

First, I acknowledged that I was afraid and allowed myself the luxury of being so, rather than trying to say, "There's nothing to be afraid of; you've had it fixed." Every time I experienced the fear, I addressed it. I asked myself, "Why am I feeling fear?" The answers would range from "I'm afraid the stents might not be working" to "I'm worried that something else could be wrong with my heart." I acknowledged that I'd been through a very serious procedure, and I listened when I was repeatedly told by people in the medical community and by those who'd had this procedure themselves that this was in fact major surgery, even though my chest hadn't been opened up. So, Step 1, I acknowledged the fear.

Next, I quantified the fear. I asked myself, on a scale of one to ten, how much fear was present. Each time I felt a twinge in my chest or thought my heart had skipped a beat, I felt a fear level of five or six.

Then I imagined the worst-case scenario. At first I thought this scenario was that I'd have a heart attack and die. However, when I remembered that I'd already confronted that possibility at the emergency room and realized that it hadn't bothered me so much, it helped to alleviate some of the fear. I also realized that I'd been closer to death and in more danger prior to having the procedure than I was after having it, so that helped alleviate some of it, too. Delving a little deeper, I realized that my "new" worst-case scenario was that I'd have to go through this again, and maybe the next time I had chest pains they'd have to open up my chest. However, I knew that, more often than not, even that procedure is successful, so that helped alleviate the fear.

Next, I gathered information and support to help me confront the perception and dissipate the fear. Each time I felt threatened or felt those twinges of pain, I'd call Dr. Koshkarian. Being the healer that he is, he'd always call me back or have his triage nurse call to assure me that the pains had nothing to do with the possibility of a breakdown of the procedure. Dr. Koshkarian and his team were available to me 24 hours a day. They walked me through those first six months until I became, and remain, totally comfortable with the fact that I'm in great health once again.

By having these tools, I was able to acknowledge the fear, quantify it, look at the worst-case scenario (oftentimes redefining it in the process), gather information, and move on. Subsequently, after six months, I was given a clean bill of health. Dr. Koshkarian told me that since there were no major problems, chances are that I'm in great shape for the life that lies ahead of me. That's when it was time for the final step: *Celebrate!*

Since that time, my health has continued to improve. My arteries are flowing optimally and are as clear as they can possibly be. It's now 2006, and I'm healthier than I was 20 years ago. I don't pay attention to every little twinge anymore. I'm taking care of myself so as not to create future episodes of heart illness. Life is good and well worth celebrating.

So, what does all this have to do with the laws of cause and effect? Well, sometime after the procedure, my doctor told me that the blockage in my heart was probably the result of years of self-destructive living with alcohol, drugs, and cigarettes. Although I'd quit smoking cigars two years earlier and been chemical free since 1979, my change of lifestyle had probably only postponed the inevitable. Since my cessation of drug use, I'd lived a life that I'd assumed was blessed, and in many ways it was. In truth, the laws of cause and effect hadn't let me get away with those years of abuse. They took their toll on my physical body, but the lessons I learned were invaluable.

I'm really glad to be alive and writing this book from a place of awareness that I wouldn't have had if I'd gotten away with something. It's just a further affirmation that accountability is necessary for us to grow, and to remember who we are.

≒✳≒

INTRODUCTION

As I BEGAN WRITING THIS BOOK, which gives you steps to apply to your life when you just don't know what to do (what I call "common horse sense"), I immediately found myself in need of those steps. Feeling scared for maybe the billionth time in my life, I asked myself what qualified me to sit down and write about a subject that I obviously hadn't resolved. I suppose I had an expectation that I would've been over my fear and self-doubt now that I've entered my sixth decade on the planet, but I guess that's just another story I made up to avoid dealing with it.

I'll probably never stop experiencing fear and self-doubt—I don't think anyone ever does. Maybe that's what qualifies me to write a book about the process of fear, the multitude of voices it has, and all the programming that goes into causing us humans to doubt ourselves. Maybe I'm qualified because I've constantly and successfully used the five steps in this book for confronting that programming on a message-by-message basis.

Does that mean I'll never be totally unafraid? Probably not. Fears and doubts will always arise. As we go through the various stages and events in life, making one transition after another, we're constantly called upon to confront new things that we've never faced before. This book is not about getting rid of *all* fear and self-doubt once and for all and never having to face these feelings again. Rather, it entails a five-step process for overcoming fear and self-doubt whenever they arise.

Part of what I'm going to talk about in this book is my perception. I'm certainly not the final word on anything, but I do know one thing for sure: For many years of my life, I was an expert on being terrified. I did everything humanly possible to try to hide that fact until it almost destroyed me. I can't remember when I didn't feel somewhat inferior to every other soul on the planet. That isn't the case anymore, so I'm living proof that some of these things can be healed. I'm in the process of healing even as we speak.

In my first book, *It's Not about the Horse,* I spoke about spending the first half of my life complicating everything I possibly could because I was so damn smart. At that point in time, I arrived at a place of realizing that I knew absolutely nothing. I had no answers. Upon realizing this, I became even more fearful than I'd ever been, but I had no map for acknowledging the fear, much less for having any idea how to deal with it, and I was extremely terrified. Only then did I realize that the answer had been there all along, and in the simplest of forms: I had to simplify my life entirely.

I'll never forget, as long as I live, how it felt when I finally was able to give myself permission to acknowledge to another human being that I was afraid, with no ulterior motive for saying it, other than to just be honest about what was going on with me. The words were "Me, too," and they were in response to having a man whom I admired acknowledge to me that he had awakened that particular morning feeling scared. I couldn't say "Me, too" fast enough. I was no longer dealing with something on my own. I had an ally, and I was no longer the most defective person on the planet. That was just a story I'd made up.

Since that time, and over the past 27 years—24 of which have been spent working, studying, and growing as a therapist—I've finally arrived at the five simple steps for overcoming fear and self-doubt. They represent nothing more than common horse sense.

Step 1: Acknowledge the fear and self-doubt. Don't minimize it, don't call it something it isn't (such as nervousness, apprehension, or anxiety). Just admit that you feel afraid or scared.

Step 2: Quantify the fear and self-doubt. On a scale of one to ten, how much fear and self-doubt are you experiencing? Once you've established a level of fear, you've acknowledged just how grave you perceive the situation to be.

Step 3: Imagine the worst-case scenario. What's the worst possible thing that could happen? It's important to admit to yourself, and ideally to another person, the story your mind has made up about the situation. Usually the worst-case scenario is: "I'll end up feeling humiliated, and I won't be able to survive, either emotionally or physically."

Step 4: Gather information and support, confront the perception, and dissipate the fear. Gather all the information and support you can with respect to coping with your worst-case scenario so it doesn't occur. Once the information and support are there, you can confront your perception. By addressing the physical situation, not only do you survive, but you're generally able to walk through the perceived difficulty. At that point, the fear automatically dissipates. You find that you're not defective and your self-doubt disappears.

Step 5: Celebrate! You've arrived in present-moment time. When you walk through your fear and self-doubt, you always end up in a place of joy.

If this seems like a lot of work, or if it seems tedious, let me assure you that it isn't nearly as much work as you'll face if you postpone doing it. I remember hearing an interview with Don Henley of the rock band the Eagles. He was asked, "How do you people, after 30 years, continue to sound as good, if not better, than you ever did?"

He said, "You have to have a tolerance for repetition."

I thought to myself, *In order to do that, you'd certainly have to believe in what you're repeating!* Well, let me tell you, I believe in this process. Every time I see it used, I see people arrive at the place in time that's their birthright. It's a place of joy. It's the joy of living that's always found on the opposite side of fear and self-doubt. There's no way to go around it, under it, or over it. It's a process, and it has to be gone through, but I can promise you that the rewards are well worth the effort.

⊰✳⊱

Chapter One

The Origins of Fear and Self-Doubt

ONE MORNING, A COUPLE OF YEARS BACK, I was gathering the participants for the Equine Experience, a workshop I lead at the Miraval Life in Balance™ resort in Tucson, Arizona. As our general manager walked past us in the lobby, I said, "So, Joseph, what's your story today?"

He looked at me and said, "Wyatt, I hate myself."

Several of the people looked at him as if he were crazy, and one gentleman asked me, "Who was that?"

I said, "That's my boss. He runs this place."

"He runs this place?" he asked incredulously. "He just said he hates himself."

"Let's try a quick experiment," I said, speaking to all ten participants who had gathered by then. "I want you to take three minutes here. The first minute and a half, I want you to write down a list of the negative things about yourself that truly need improvement."

I gave them all pencils and paper and began timing them as they worked diligently on their lists. At the conclusion of a minute and a half, I said, "Now write down those things about you that, if we knew about them, would make us be in awe of you. List the things that would make us stand up and applaud with admiration in our eyes."

Once again, I started timing them. This time, instead of writing busily, they began to look at me repeatedly and seemed a little nervous. At the end of the minute and a half, I asked one question: "Which list is longer?"

Silence fell upon the room, and a couple of people said, "The first one, of course."

Of course?

Joseph had provided a wonderful opportunity for us that morning, a window into the world of fear and self-doubt. If I look at how it feels to experience those emotions, I believe that they translate into two things: one is that we hate ourselves; the other is that we're afraid someone else might see what we see and hate us, too. Is that extreme? Of course, but when we get right down to the very core of fear and self-doubt, that's how it feels. I believe that this feeling is a misperception, certainly, but it's one that many of us have had for most of our lives.

According to how we've been trained, it seems to be easier to criticize than it is to praise—and that's the problem. We've been trained to hate ourselves, and the only salvation we can hope to come up with is to correct that misperception so we'll believe that we're worth saving. How do we correct the misperception? By walking through the fear and self-doubt.

First Things First

Before we go much further, let's examine those terms a little more closely.

Webster's Collegiate Dictionary defines *fear* as "an unpleasant, often strong emotion caused by anticipation or awareness of danger; an instance of this emotion; a state marked by this emotion; anxious concern; reason for alarm: DANGER." I wonder on a daily basis, as I work with clients, how much fear is based on actual, immediate danger. Yes, there's anticipation. And yes, there are the stories we make up about danger being imminent, yet in reality it usually isn't.

When I looked for the term *self-doubt* in the dictionary, I couldn't find it. I found *self-despair, self-destruction, self-determination, self-evident, self-examination, self-executing, self-explanatory,* and *self-explanation,* but no *self-doubt.* I don't know why, but I find that kind of ironic and somewhat unbelievable. So I went to *self* and then to *doubt,* and put the two together.

The definitions of *self* include "the entire person of an individual; an individual's typical character or behavior." *Doubt* is defined as "to lack confidence in; distrust; an inclination not to believe or accept." Combining them, self-doubt truly is a lack of acceptance of the self. In an externally focused world, where values are seen as coming from the external, if we had self-doubt, we'd probably be afraid that someone might find out. So there it is. The world is set up to function as a self-winding system of fear and self-doubt.

Fear, Self-Doubt, and the Systems That Create Them

On a daily basis, we walk through the world influenced by various systems, all of which appear to be based in, and run by, self-doubt and fear. There are systems of reward and punishment, well beyond what the natural law calls for. There is win/lose. There is right/wrong. There is bad/good. There are systems that pay lip service to us as individuals but discount our work and our worth for the good of the system. In such a culture, it's impossible for every one of us to feel good about ourselves, because on a daily basis someone has to lose. It's crazy.

Let's take a look at some of these systems and how they operate in our culture.

PATRIARCHAL SYSTEMS

It seems to me that eons ago, maybe one or two men got together, men of power (or perceived power in those days), and began to make up a set of rules. Maybe they hoped to gain the support of their tribe, or maybe they wanted to exert power over a group of people. Here I am, making up stories again, but it seems that our culture has been patriarchal for hundreds and hundreds of years. The rules seem to have been written by scared men for the purpose of gaining control of the culture.

I know that in present-day culture the rules haven't changed much since I was a boy, and that was 60 years ago. To this day, it's not okay for men to be afraid. It's not okay for men to be sensitive, to acknowledge their pain. It's not okay for women to be angry or powerful, because this seems to scare men. It seems that the only acceptable feeling in this culture is happiness, but nobody tells us how to get there. Maybe we need to learn how to deal with whatever is perceived in the culture as having power and therefore frightening to us.

RELIGIOUS SYSTEMS

If we look at the cultural norms that permeate our systems, most of them seem to have come from basic religious systems, which are set up according to the concepts of right and wrong, or a belief that there's a right way and a wrong way to do something. I truly think that a lot of the self-doubt and fear that have been perpetuated, certainly upon Western civilization, have come from the Judeo-Christian systems found in organized religion.

If we look at the creation theory of how the world began, we find two people hanging out in Paradise. The story goes that they're naked and quite happy that way—totally innocent and wanting for nothing. Of course, being a universe of duality, the flip side of this occurs in the form of the serpent that manages to get to the "weaker sex."

I'm sure that men wrote the Bible. I don't think women had a damn thing to do with it, because the very first chapter placed all the responsibility for what happened to the world upon the serpent and the woman. God, how horrible! When Eve was supposedly seduced by the serpent into eating from the Tree of Knowledge, and then offered Adam a bite, their first thought wasn't, *Oh, my God! Fruit is a horrible thing.* No, it had nothing to do with fruit. The most horrible thing that could have happened for them was to realize, *Oh my God—we're naked! Being naked is a bad thing.* They felt instant body shame. Imagine—a belief that the body was shameful appears in the first few pages of the best-selling book in the history of humankind. Talk about fear and self-doubt!

If this belief system has anything to do with what God intended for us, I don't get it. Why would God tell us to cover ourselves up? Focus externally? Reinvent what we look like, because what we look like is horrible and bad? Decorate our bodies as much as we can, because what's underneath is a shameful thing?

Immediate self-doubt and the fear of its discovery were instituted and saturated throughout the teachings of the Judeo-Christian religions. I believe this is where they came from. I know they did for me. In my first book, I talked about feeling horribly guilty for having sexual feelings. I also remember being told, "If you think it, you might as well have done it." What children on this planet can control what they think? How are they supposed to feel about themselves if they're breaking God's laws, minute by minute, as a result of what they're thinking? Even the most advanced minds in the world don't have a hell of a lot of control over their thoughts. We all have choices, but to expect that of children is a horrible thing.

I remember viewing one of the nature channels a few years back and seeing a tribe that hadn't been, at that time, discovered by Western civilization. They were nomads who lived off herbs and monkeys. They were naked, and they were the happiest-looking people I've ever seen in my life. They had absolutely no body shame. Unfortunately, we've probably civilized them by now, and screwed them up eight ways from Sunday.

OUR SYSTEM OF COMPETITION

Patriarchal and religious systems aren't the only systems that lead to fear and self-doubt. Anytime we walk out into the culture, and certainly where I live, in the United States of America, the competition is on: Somebody needs to win and somebody needs to lose.

In our Western culture, it appears that the primary means of securing material wealth is our system of competition. I'm glad I live in a capitalistic nation. I enjoy nice things, and I think money's fun, but our beliefs about money are making us sick.

How can a system where only the few can win, perpetuate wholeness, happiness, and a sense of peace? I watch people in relationships continually competing with each other. Closeness is over when that happens. The same is true when it comes to money.

Most of the people in the world are not dramatically rich, which is what *successful* often means in our culture. The rest of us can see ourselves as losers if we believe in the system, and the system is thrown at us in millions of ways. Just about everything that's advertised in order to make money is set up to compare one standard against another, and most of these standards are totally unrealistic. We need to wear a certain kind of hat or a particular brand of shoes. Only two or three nice automobiles symbolize success. There's something crazy about a system that defines goodness and success this way.

I've met a lot of people who believed in the system and wound up very sad. I've also met a lot of people who worked through the system—they didn't work *for* the money, but they made incredible amounts of money and knew what to do with it. They found their greatest happiness in the process of giving.

Money itself is not a bad thing. When fear and self-doubt cause us to believe that *we* are a bad thing, we tend to look outside ourselves and create a standard based on material value. That standard is destined to disappoint us. As I've said before, the only standard that will bring us joy and happiness is to eliminate the fear and self-doubt so that we might experience the joy that is our birthright. That doesn't happen through the systems of competition that we've created in the world. It certainly doesn't seem to have happened so far.

FAMILY SYSTEMS

All of the systems I've described so far, in my opinion, grow from family systems, most of which are dysfunctional in nature. The dysfunctional family system says, "Don't talk, don't trust, don't feel." We can walk into any corporate system in America and experience that on a daily basis. The larger systems are nothing more than an extension of the smaller systems.

What happens when we confront or go up against the major systems in any way? Generally, we risk being labeled, and rarely are we labeled in a favorable way. The labels are usually discounting, degrading, or punishing. For example, if we confront the governmental systems, we can be labeled anarchists or traitors. If we confront the religious systems, we're generally referred to as heathens, nonbelievers, or sinners, and we're likely to be expelled from their midst. If we confront the corporate system, we may be labeled as troublemakers or people who aren't team players, and we put ourselves at risk of losing our jobs. And if we confront the family system, we may be used as scapegoats or labeled as disloyal, as traitors, or as people who don't love or who betray.

Living, Not Just Surviving

If we can't confront the systems without becoming labeled, lonely outcasts, how in the world are we supposed to survive? It seems that we generally have to succumb to the system and be subjugated to its rules. But this is not about just surviving. The real question is, how do we *live* within these systems?

11

Regardless of the type of system, or the consequences for confronting or stepping outside of it, I
believe we'll pay a higher price if we *don't* question
the system. How are we ever to have our own personal integrity if we don't question what we're told
and taught by these various institutions? More important, how can they ever hope to heal and improve
themselves?

The original system that has to be dealt with is
ourselves—yourself or myself as an independent system. What kinds of rules are we willing to live by?
What type of value system do we have? Is our value
system important enough for us to enforce and honor
these rules, to develop our own system of bylaws or
ethics—things that we will not compromise? If we're
willing to do these types of things, we ultimately
can live, as opposed to just survive. Generally speaking, the path to that place is through a process of
being willing to be labeled, willing to be alone, willing to be an outcast, willing to seek the truth. The
only way to get to that place is through a process of
deprogramming.

We've been programmed by all of these external
conglomerates called systems. So, how do we confront the systems and deprogram ourselves? We must
start by questioning everything we've ever been told
in our lives to see if it holds up under our scrutiny.

If it doesn't, chances are it's bogus and needs to be discarded or ignored. The information that does hold up to scrutiny can be utilized to enhance the quality of our lives. In order to reach this place—this present-moment time—we have to walk through our fear and the subsequent self-doubt that accompanies it.

The arrival into present-moment time takes place in the realm of emotional and spiritual systems. In Western society, this is not where we typically spend the majority of our time. Instead, we seem to be enmeshed with family, corporate, religious, and governmental systems that are, for the most part, designed to keep us out of present-moment time and to devalue the individual.

I'm not here to question anyone's religious beliefs; certainly, it's none of my business what anyone believes religiously or otherwise. I'm not here to try to change corporate America. I'm not here to be a naysayer for the capitalistic system that we live in and from which I surely benefit. I'm also not here to be an authority on how any family system should be run. As I put this book together, I simply looked for a way to express how I feel about systems in general, without presenting myself as a person who has the answers to the problems with these systems, because I don't. I just feel the need to express what I'm left with as I try to make sense of them. Generally speaking,

I'm left with a sense of sadness and disappointment, with a bit of anger thrown in.

For the life of me, I can't comprehend why anyone on this planet should starve to death. I look at the homeless people walking the streets of America, and that just doesn't make sense to me at all. Religious institutions are housed in buildings that cost millions of dollars, while people are homeless and hungry. It doesn't make sense on a moral or a spiritual level. It's absolutely insane.

I was in Boston recently, in the month of January. It was very cold, and I read in the newspaper that people were living in homemade tents on the outskirts of the city. I passed a Salvation Army center and saw what appeared to be upwards of 100 coats and other types of warm clothing lying at the door for people who didn't have a comfortable place to be in such weather. Once again, crazy.

Sometime back, my wife, Carin, showed me a very small belt, about 30 inches long. It wasn't lined, it looked like water buffalo, and it cost $200. I used to donate to a charity that would feed a child for $16 a month—for the price of that belt, I could've fed a child for 12 months.

I read what some corporate systems spend on 30 seconds of commercial advertising time during the Super Bowl every year. This staggering amount of money could probably feed three-fourths of the people who are hungry in one of our major cities. It certainly could build housing for people who might be cold. I'm quite sure that a lot of these corporations give tons of money to causes like this, but as long as there's one hungry child, or one cold man or woman on the street, maybe our attention should go there first. It appears that we have our priorities screwed up.

I'm not saying that I have the answers to how to do it or how to cure it, I'm just saying that it saddens me when I see it. I don't understand how this can happen, other than that it does so with our permission. Until we refuse to allow this to occur, people will continue to be hungry and will continue to freeze to death.

I no longer believe that the decision to walk through our fear and self-doubt can be made by groups as large as entire communities, states, countries, or continents. I believe it has to happen one individual at a time, and that's the purpose of this book. I hope to show this journey in such a way that maybe one, two, or three people will decide to confront their fear and self-doubt. Every time one of us does so, we prove that it's possible for others, and the ripple effect can be quite dramatic. I think we've long been dissatisfied; and we have to be courageous enough to give voice to our dissatisfaction, certainly in an individual way, and be willing to change our individual worlds. On a daily basis, each of us moves in a 150-square-foot area at any given moment. We're certainly influenced by other people who bring their world into our space. Why not try to influence others as well?

Looking for Heroes in All the Wrong Places

I'm convinced that one of the major causes of fear and self-doubt is that we don't have a functional, healthy system in place for dealing with how we feel. We aren't taught how to deal with fear and anger, where these emotions even come from, or how to deal with shame. When we can't deal with what we feel, we end up feeling crazy, and *crazy* is a bad word in this culture. It means being out of touch with reality, scattered, or irrational.

If we're willing to look at this in depth, we can change it. I am, this very day, trying to change my world. It's a small world, but if I change a little part of it and you change a little part of yours, and someone who sees us decides to change, too, the change just spreads and continues to grow. We've seen repeated instances of this throughout our history. Unfortunately, we've often turned these simple, humble people who've done these things into heroes. We say, "I could never do what they did," and we become in awe of them because of how we feel about ourselves.

It seems to me that heroes are simply people who can work through their fear and do whatever it takes to achieve their dreams—even if it means dying for what they believe in. In other words, they know how to transcend their fear and self-doubt. They're people of faith and conviction. Why don't we see ourselves as those kinds of people? I believe it's partially because of the way our culture promotes and treats heroes.

How many times and in how many ways have we been told to be like someone else, dress for success, or follow some other suggestion that translates into "being ordinary isn't enough"? Our culture promotes hero worship at an intense level by spending millions and millions of dollars on media, sports, and movie heroes. This has gone on throughout history, and it continues to be done on a daily basis. Yet, at the same time, we seem to do everything we can to lay a trap for those celebrity heroes. When they meet our expectations and rise to the top, what do we do? We tear them down! I suspect that we do this because we find out that turning other people into heroes doesn't fill up the hole in our soul, so we try to destroy them. This is nothing more than the story of how we treat ourselves, but instead of realizing that, we focus externally and we just don't get it.

As a young boy, I always wanted to be like someone else. I remember wanting to be like my older brother. He was my hero. We need to ask ourselves why we'd want to be like anyone else. Whose idea was it, anyway?

I'm pretty sure this whole concept of heroes gets its start in the family system. Our mothers and fathers set themselves up as heroes, telling us, "We're the ones you need. We can save you, keep you safe, and take great pride in that." When we get out of the family system, Mom and Dad are no longer there, but we've been programmed to look for someone to tell us what to do. I don't know very many people who grew up in systems where the parents said, "Don't ever sacrifice who you are in order to be like someone else. You're so special that if you just nurture that soul, there's no telling what might happen. There is where the magic of life is." Mostly we're told, "Why don't you be like so-and-so? Look at him or her."

When we're actively involved in wanting to be like someone else, we're actually saying that who we are isn't enough. We're saying that, in and of ourselves, we aren't good enough to meet some standard. It seems to me that the only reason we'd ever need external heroes is because we believed that we weren't capable of being heroes ourselves, because we believed that we were flawed rather than heroic.

What do we call our heroes? Superman or Superwoman. We make "Ordinary Man" and "Ordinary Woman" about as special as a wart on a hog. This has to stop in order for us to self-actualize. In my opinion, there's no such thing as an ordinary being. Every day, I see extraordinary things done by extraordinary people.

In order for us to remember who we are, to feel empowered, to have any hope of growing and finding the joy that certainly is our birthright, we have to discover and find worth in who we actually are. Who we are has nothing to do with what we do. It has to do with our values, our sense of personal ethics, and our self as a system with all of its needs, wants, and dreams.

I don't know that any of the people I've admired in my life could have lived in my body and gone through the things that I've gone through, with as much tenacity and integrity as I've shown, and I'm sure the same is true for all of us. Everyone has their own journey to travel. I know that's true. To say that someone else could have done better than we have is something we should never say without investigating the very depth of the strength that we possess.

This idea of turning other people into heroes has to go away. We each have to become our own hero. In my first book, I spoke about the hero's journey that I heard about early on from writer and anthropologist Joseph Campbell. We are each involved in that journey in our daily lives, and it is not to be taken lightly, nor is it a journey for sissies. If we are to discover—or *remember*—who we are, and to find worth in that, we have to take the journey into the darkest parts of our fear and self-doubt and correct those misperceptions. We have to become our own heroes and walk into our own darkness, confront our own perceived dragons, and come out on the other side with the dragons and the darkness as our strongest allies. When that happens, we give hope to anybody who's watching because we show that it's possible.

Maria's Story

Maria was in her late 40s or early 50s when she came to participate in the Equine Experience. Her story shows the powerful impact a system can have.

As I always do at the start of the program, I sat down to talk with Maria and the other six people in her group under a shady canopy in front of the arena where they'd soon be working with the horses. As my staff led the horses into the arena, I talked a little bit about what we'd be doing and asked each participant to tell us about themselves.

As Maria spoke, we learned that this divorced mother of an 18-year-old son was absolutely exhausted. Her body hurt continuously, with the most extensive pain occurring from her lower back all the way up to the base of her skull. She'd been raised in Mexico City in an affluent family, but fled them to come to America because of the repressive culture she experienced as a Mexican female. She'd felt that women were seen as unequal, not as good as men, and therefore denied the opportunities that a man would have.

When she came to this country, Maria believed she'd have to do better than anyone else because of the language barrier, because she was a woman, and because she was entering "a man's world." Clearly, she brought her history with her before even investigating the emotional and physical landscape here in the States. Despite those perceived barriers, Maria eventually worked her way to the position of executive vice president in charge of financial development in a prominent American corporation.

When Maria finished her story and everyone else had taken their turns to speak, we left the canopy area and entered the arena with the horses. Standing with the group, I described the various tasks each person would have the opportunity to perform. In the Equine Experience, each participant is paired with a horse. We show them how to safely approach it and give it a cue to raise its front hoof. Their job is to clean the hoof, do the same with the back leg, then brush and comb that side of the horse. Next, they'll carefully walk around the horse and repeat the process on the other side, and finally they'll untie the horse from the fence and lead it around the arena, using their body language to direct the animal.

As we went over the routine, Maria had more questions for me than any client I've worked with in a group situation in the last five to ten years. She asked about the tasks involved and possible safety concerns, but mostly she wanted to know how to "succeed." Success for her meant achieving the tasks and doing so before anyone else could. She had a desperate need to win. She was one of the most fear-based people I'd met in quite some time, and much of her fear was based on her own history and the stories that she'd made up about what she brought to the group on this particular day.

As she began to work with her horse, Maria was extremely tentative with every move she made. She petted the horse in an exaggerated manner and spoke to him in high-pitched, baby-talk tones. This, as is quite often the case, led to the horse ignoring her and eventually going to sleep. Maria tried again to gain the horse's cooperation, but he only ignored her again. By the time I walked over to her, she looked terrified. It was the perfect opportunity to utilize the five steps for overcoming fear and self-doubt.

First, I asked Maria what she was feeling, and she was able to admit that she was, in fact, afraid. When I asked her to quantify the level of fear she was experiencing in that moment, she gave it a nine out of a possible ten on the fear scale. Next, I asked her, "What's the worst possible thing that could happen?"

She replied, "The horse won't cooperate. I'll feel terrible about myself, and everyone will know that I'm not capable."

At that point in time, I helped Maria with Step 4 by giving her some information. I pointed out that the rest of the group was involved with their own endeavors and that nobody was watching her except her and whomever she brought with her in her mind.

As we continued to work, Maria was unable to access any type of emotions at a level any deeper than just below the surface. She had no framework for feeling any part of this history. She had pretty much separated from any part of her that could have been vulnerable. She was totally working in her head and was glued to the cultural wounds that she'd brought to this country with her.

I asked her if her fear ever manifested itself in any other way than self-criticism. She talked about anger coming up for her and how she'd used it for years as a way of coping with her feelings of inadequacy and the fear of being found out for feeling such a thing. She told me that she never let anyone know she was angry; it was a secret weapon for her. As I looked at her, I knew that this woman had deluded herself. Her anger was quite obvious. In fact, the reason I'd asked her about it in the first place was because I hadn't seen her smile once since we'd gathered with the group that morning.

Maria admitted, "I never smile."

When I asked her why, she stated that she refused to get her needs met by flirting. This woman had been treated poorly for being a female and had pretty much taken the warrior stance as a way of conducting her life. I encouraged her to use her anger openly—not to be aggressive toward the horse, not to be critical of herself, but as a source of energy for her. I assured her that not all cultures in the world were going to be punitive toward her for using her anger as energy. I don't think this woman knew what anger was. She'd repressed it for so many years that she'd lost the choice of using it as energy and was at its mercy when it manifested as rage. I asked her to get focused on herself, and she was able to do so.

In doing what I asked, Maria had begun to take instruction from a powerful male and had stopped competing with me. All of a sudden, she seemed softer. She'd finally given herself permission to do something other than what she'd always done, which really wasn't working for her. When that happened, the horse began to cooperate.

I then asked her about her body and the pain she was experiencing. I asked whether she now felt a little more loose and comfortable in her body, and when she stated that she did, she smiled for the first time. This woman had a great smile! I acknowledged how beautiful her smile was and encouraged her to use it more often because it looked nice on her. I told her it was very clear to me that she wasn't flirting with me or anybody else, and that a smile of joy was a wonderful thing.

Maria completed her tasks and continued to soften as the process went on. We'd gone all the way through the five steps for overcoming fear and self-doubt. She'd identified the fear, quantified it, talked about the worst-case scenario, and in a roundabout way, tapped in to getting some information about how to avoid the worst case. Finally, she had, without knowing it, moved beyond being at the mercy of her fear and self-doubt all the way to a place of smiling for the first time in quite a while, which was a modicum of celebration—but I was hoping for more.

We then moved on to our next exercise, where each participant takes turns working with a single horse in the center of a 60-foot-wide round pen. Using nothing but body language and a training whip similar to the ones used by lion tamers and ringmasters, I showed them how to guide the horse around the perimeter of the round pen, causing it to speed up, slow down, turn around, and stop. I demonstrated how to use the whip (it's never used to strike the animals) and position the body at various angles to communicate with the horse.

When it was Maria's turn, she kept getting ahead of the horse. She couldn't seem to stay at the correct angle to give him clear direction to go forward, so of course the horse stood still. Maria stopped in the middle of the round pen and asked, "Is this horse stopping because I'm continually getting ahead of it?"

When I assured her that this was definitely the case, she announced, "Oh, my God! This is how I live my life. I get ahead of myself, things don't go well, and then I'm really hard on myself."

I explained to Maria and the rest of the group that the things we learn early in life that drive us, push us, and give us physical and material success in the world are often the coping skills of children. They help create a degree of safety and reward for us, but later on in life they become a block to our happiness. Maria was able to understand this at a level that heretofore had not been possible.

Continuing to work with Maria in the round pen, I gave her specific instructions and told her that her true commitment was not to get ahead of the horse's front shoulder. That's all I wanted her to pay attention to, and I asked if she'd be willing to do that. She did, and the horse worked as smoothly as I could have worked him, changing gaits from walk to trot to canter and back, as I encouraged Maria and gave her small suggestions. Each time the horse cooperated, Maria would break into laughter. The smile had turned into laughter.

After Maria had worked the horse for about four minutes, I asked her to drop the whip, take a deep breath, and let it out. When she did, the horse immediately stopped and turned toward her. She continued to laugh out loud, and I explained that she'd just taken the fifth step for overcoming fear and self-doubt: total celebration. I pointed out that she'd worked herself to this place simply by being willing to confront a lifetime of conditioning. I couldn't help but remind her that, even though she hadn't smiled in years, she'd smiled at least eight times in the last five minutes, at which point she laughed again. We began to explore the possibility of there being an endless supply of laughter and joy directly at the other end of the tenacity associated with her fear and self-doubt.

She looked at me and asked, "Do you really think that's possible?"

I told her that not only was it possible, it was a law, because we live in a universe of duality, of cause and effect.

As we sat down with the group to process the events of the day, Maria began to see how her fears and self-doubts had affected all aspects of her life. She talked about being so fearful every time her son drove her car that she required him to check in every hour to make sure he was okay. She talked about her need for control, and how she now realized that she was totally *out* of control while living in an illusion of being *in* control. She talked about having a total fear of flying, and suddenly realized that it was actually a fear of not piloting the plane. She was afraid of having someone else in charge of any part of her life, and she now realized that it was related to her history, a trauma-based familial and cultural setting of spiritual deprivation and repression.

As our time together neared its end, Maria made an agreement with the group that for the next six months she would get a massage a week. She asked if I thought it would help. I let her in on an important lesson that had been shared with me some 24 years ago: "What do you have to lose?"

She looked at me and said, "Maybe some of this pain."

I asked if her pain was better, if it had been relieved as the day had gone on. With a beautiful smile, which by now was as present as the frown had been when she first showed up, she shrugged her shoulders and indicated that it had indeed been greatly relieved.

The change that occurred on that particular July day in 105-degree heat in Tucson was in direct relationship to Maria's willingness to do something different and to avail herself of the five steps for overcoming fear and self-doubt. She had truly arrived in present-moment time, where she received her inheritance of joy.

❄❄❄

Chapter Two

Breaking Out of a
Self-Imposed Prison

THE FIRST STEP AND PERHAPS THE MOST IMPORTANT part of overcoming fear and self-doubt is to acknowledge that they exist. It's impossible to begin the journey without acknowledging that we're afraid, or that we feel faulty or defective. As soon as we acknowledge our fear, the secret is out and the journey begins. Until that happens, fear and self-doubt lie within—festering, turning our emotional bodies to stone; and often destroying us physically with anger, shame, and those kinds of things that will certainly manifest themselves as disease later on in our lives. Until we deal with these ravaging emotions, we sentence ourselves to a self-imposed prison, both spiritual and emotional, which will eventually turn into a physical prison. We make ourselves sick by first contributing to our own spiritual and emotional disease. I cannot overemphasize the importance of acknowledging fear and self-doubt.

So, how do we eliminate fear and self-doubt? I believe it takes nothing more than willingness. We don't have to know what we're doing. We don't have to believe that dealing with fear and self-doubt is going to help, or even that we can deal with it. We just have to know that we're presently coming from a place of fear and self-doubt, and it's not what we want. We begin to unlock the prison doors by seeing that fear and self-doubt are a means of *existing* in the world, not *living,* and they don't work. *Existing* is merely survival, and it's a struggle. It's painful and it hurts. When we get tired enough of that, we're generally willing to take suggestions and help from others. That's what it takes to set ourselves free.

A Global Wake-Up Call

I'm deeply concerned about whether or not we as a species change, and I'm concerned about how fast that happens. I watch, on a daily basis, as we continue to be in conflict about the same things, over and over again. We're fighting wars today for the same reasons we fought them 40 or 50 years ago. I believe it's because we keep refusing to deal with our fear and self-doubt. We refuse to take responsibility for our own lives because, in order to do so, we'd have to look at what we think and feel as the genesis and driving force behind our energy systems. (What we think and feel dictates our behavior.)

I often tell the people I work with that I'm not even trying to be happy anymore as I live my day-to-day life. I'm just trying to get sane. I believe that happiness is a by-product of sanity. On a daily basis, we continue to follow the old layman's definition of insanity: doing the same thing over and over and expecting different results. I think we're just walking around being crazy, and I think it's because we're afraid to be sane. I think we're afraid to take responsibility for our lives. At this point and time, we seem to think there's no other choice.

I look at our world systems much like I've looked at addictive systems. Being an addict and an alcoholic was certainly a curse and almost killed me, but it also gave me life and was a blessing. The microcosm of addictive disease has given me a framework for looking at the macrocosm of how we're treating our planet right now. Just like the addicts who use drugs or alcohol to feel good for a while but ultimately poison their bodies, we've discovered some things in life that bring us short-term benefits and long-term problems. Our fast cars give us fun and excitement while they spew out pollutants that poison the earth. We've produced products that look good, feel good, taste good, and give us a huge rush, but after a while they become ineffective. So we need more, more— nothing's ever enough. It reminds me of something I learned from a man named Herb.

I met Herb at a 12-step meeting, where he talked about being grateful that he was an alcoholic. At the time, I thought he was crazy. He certainly looked a little crazy. He reminded me of Jiggs, the character in the comic strip "Maggie and Jiggs" that ran in the papers when I was a kid. Jiggs had hair that stuck out on both sides, and Herb looked just like him. He was a short, fat guy, and he was absolutely brilliant, like the nutty professor himself. Herb was a lawyer, and he talked about money. He'd say, "I always wanted more, and when I got it, all I had was some." That seems to be exactly what we've done as a culture: We've chased after more, more, more, but we've only come up empty and filled with pain.

In describing the process of addictive disease, self-help groups know that when addicts eventually create enough pain for themselves, one of three things will happen: They'll be locked up, covered up, or sobered up. In terms of what we're doing to this planet, we seem to be somewhere in the midst of being locked up and covered up. Species are becoming extinct. We're depleting our resources. The ozone layer is being destroyed while we ignore it and chase after "progress." We've created prisons for ourselves emotionally, spiritually, and ecologically. If the world was an alcoholic, the "powers that be" would surely be considering an intervention right now.

I guess if I could sum it all up, I wonder if we're going to wake up in time. If we don't, Mother Earth will reclaim herself. If we stay asleep long enough, we'll create weapons that will blow us up, we'll poison our air, and we've already damn near destroyed our drinking water. We're poisoning ourselves as fast as we can. Many homes already have air purifiers in them, and we've been buying bottled water for years. Rather than taking responsibility for what we've done and trying to reverse that, we just invent more gadgets to postpone the inevitable—and we call it progress. It's absolutely crazy!

If we don't stop, we'll eventually destroy ourselves. Mother Earth will find a way to reclaim herself. As arrogant as we are as a species (and arrogance usually rises from fear and self-doubt), I truly believe that if we're willing to deal with our problems, we might become teachable so that we can see what we're doing and possibly change. If we as a culture could stop locking up and covering up and start sobering up, things could be reversed. I've repeatedly seen myself and others create prisons for themselves, hit bottom, and almost die before we woke up in time to make drastic changes and do something different. I've watched so-called hopeless individuals and groups change their entire lives to the point of being called miraculous. As a world culture, I know we can do it, too. I believe that we can create the miracle of recovering the earth and bringing peace and joy to our planet.

If we could go back to acknowledging that we as individuals are systems, and if enough of us were to participate in the miracle of change, then the bigger systems around us would be forced to change as well. I don't want to sound like some sort of pessimist, but just about all the behavior I see in every system I witness is based in fear. I wonder how many times a day we don't speak our truth—our own belief systems—because of the fear of how we might be perceived. What might it cost us within our current systems? Would we lose the respect of others? Would someone not like us as much if we kept our mouths shut? Would it cost us our jobs? Would it cost us financially to speak our minds?

I think that withholding our truth and not speaking our minds is the same as committing spiritual suicide. I watch people every day walking around pissed off because they don't know how to do anything else.

This fear that we won't be liked if we get real has been confirmed for me several times in my life. A great teacher years ago said, "Cast not your pearls before swine." To me, this suggests that we ought to be discerning about whom we offer our best to, but by all means, we need to offer our best. Why can't we just sit down and be real with each other? Why can't we just say precisely what's on our mind without feeling threatened? The answer is fear and self-doubt. We're so afraid that someone won't like us that we don't even put ourselves out there to find out.

As I discussed this with my friend and editor, Gail Fink, she told me something that made a lot of sense. She said, "I think it's a lot like fishing. Sometimes you cast your line and you get nothing. Sometimes you cast your line and you catch a prize fish. If you never throw your line out there, you'll never catch a thing. The point is to keep baiting the hook and casting your line."

The worst-case scenario is that nobody's willing to fish, that everybody's sitting around withholding because they're afraid and nobody wants to go first. In order to broaden the extent of the conversation, we have to be willing to go first at some point.

Every time I've watched somebody allow themselves to be seen in their most genuine, authentic way—to be the one to go first—I've noticed that people who are also on the same path are automatically drawn to them. Those who are extremely scared will often run from them, but mostly their authenticity gives other people permission to come a little closer. We're lonesome because we're scared. We're defensive because we're scared, and we're afraid somebody might find out who we really are. We want people to come closer, but we push them away as fast as we can. I've been doing it my whole life, and I see us doing it as a world culture, too.

If we were able to incorporate the five steps for overcoming fear and self-doubt, we'd all become good fishermen and be willing to cast our true, authentic selves out there. We'd all be willing to go first. We'd also all be willing to go second, third, and fourth. Only fear causes us to hold back. Twenty-six years ago, I read a quote in a book that has been very important to me. The book was *Twelve Steps and Twelve Traditions by* Alcoholics Anonymous, and it said: "Willingness is the key that unlocks the door to faith that works."

Melody's Story

This next story is lengthy, but I'm including it because it shows how fear can incapacitate a human being. It also shows what happens when we're willing to change—when we acknowledge, work with, and access the power of the human spirit and its ability to heal.

Melody was a woman in her early 50s who came to my attention during her four-day stay at Miraval. When I first met her, she was at least 40 pounds overweight and walked with a pronounced limp. She was attending the Equine Experience with her sister, who had won a trip to the resort and invited her along.

Many years earlier, Melody had had a terrible experience with horses and was terrified of them. I quickly learned that she was terrified of just about everything, and had been for most of her life. Despite the fact that she'd been given opportunities to talk about her history and her childhood in general, she'd never felt safe enough to do so until this particular day at Miraval. For some reason, Melody immediately felt safe when she came down to the area where we began the session.

As we sat together with the rest of the group, for the first time in her life, Melody began to talk about being terrified. She described her first childhood memory, which occurred around the age of three and which she'd kept secret for 49 years. She'd never told anyone, and until that moment, she'd been a prisoner of her own fear.

It was just beginning to snow, she remembered, when she found herself talking to her favorite teddy bear. That day, she made a serious vow to this stuffed animal that she would never hurt anyone the way her mother and sister had hurt her. Sitting under the canopy at Miraval, Melody told us that her sister was very nice now, but when their mother was alive, in order for her sister to survive, she'd sided with the mother and was a co-participant in abusing Melody Her mother was verbally abusive from day one, and Melody believed that the constant belittling, teasing, taunting, and put-downs were at the root of many of her problems.

I asked Melody what kinds of things her mother had said, and she remembered hearing things like, "You're stupid, you're dirty, you should be ashamed of yourself." She went on to say that every remark that came out of her mother's mouth was shaming toward her, but that her father had loved her very much. In fact, she was seen as "Daddy's little girl," which only infuriated her mother more.

Melody believed that her mother was jealous of her relationship with her father, even though nothing unnatural went on between them. The father was very loving, never spoke abusively, and certainly never touched her in an inappropriate fashion. Melody believed that because her father loved her so much, this caused her mother to hate her equally as much.

As I spoke with Melody, her apparent awareness of family systems showed that she had educated herself over the years. She explained that the first child, her sister, was a girl. Melody, the second child, got the message from her mother that she was the wrong sex, that it would have been better if she'd been born a boy. She said she knew her mother was thinking that she'd have to go through another pregnancy.

Melody told me that the verbal abuse went on into her adolescence, young adulthood, and even into her adult life, continuing until the day her mother died. She said that if she'd told her mother she'd gone to Miraval and that it was so nice and people were kind to her, her mother would instinctively say something like, "Of course they were nice. That's why it's so expensive." Anytime someone showed Melody kindness, her mother would say things like, "Of course people talk to you. They want you to come back because they want your money." In her late teens and early adulthood, Melody was very pretty and popular. Her mother told her that the only reason people talked to her was because she was pretty and she "put out."

At age eight, Melody was left alone in the house to wait for the gas man to come fix the furnace. The gas man did come, and he raped her. At about that time, at this very early age, she began to experience her menstrual cycle. When her mother found out, she called her a slut. Melody never told anyone about the rape until she was approximately 21 years old. When she finally did, her mother said, "We knew it all along. You probably asked for it."

Melody also related that she was so terrified as a child that, from age 3 all the way up to age 13, she'd become so fearful that she'd eventually vomit in public. She talked about how abusive the other kids would be when it happened, and that even though she had no control over it, she felt horribly defective. Her fear had taken her over physically and literally made her sick.

One day at age 13, Melody threw up in class and was taunted and made fun of by the children. From that point forward, she made a conscious decision that she would never throw up again. That was about 40 years ago, and she hasn't vomited since. She also made a conscious decision to shut her body down so that she wouldn't feel. She developed the ability to separate her thought process in such a way as to ignore the signals her body was giving her. In other words, this woman could go into a trance at will. This is symptomatic of a condition known as a dissociative disorder, and it was just one of the many sophisticated survival skills she'd created over the years in order to avoid her emotional pain.

When I asked Melody, on a scale of one to ten, how much fear she experienced on a daily basis in the first 50 years of her life, she said it was a nine. I believe that if she hadn't learned to dissociate from her feelings and find a creative way of suppressing that fear, she truly would have succumbed. When I told her how creative she was to be able to deal with something so uncontrollable without a "toolbox" at her disposal, she was moved to tears. Until that moment, she'd always looked at herself as defective, not creative, and she just thought she'd gotten lucky.

Melody's life improved until her mid-30s because of her popularity. Then, when she was 34, she experienced a horrible accident. She'd developed some sort of infection that led to pneumonia, and she was running a fever of 107 degrees and higher. She called both her mother and her sister to let them know she was very sick and to ask them for their help.

Her mother's reply was, "Well, you've always been a problem to me, and now this. You're going to have to deal with it yourself."

Her sister told her, "Don't call me. I'm fucking my husband."

The fever continued, and Melody began to hallucinate. She remembers being in her second-floor apartment, believing that the apartment was on fire and that she had to get out. Although there was no fire, she climbed out on the balcony and fell 35 feet to the ground, where she was knocked unconscious. The next morning, she was found outside the apartment window with a fever of 108 degrees, and she remained in a coma for approximately three weeks.

That fall from the balcony brought about massive amounts of suffering that lasted for the next 17 years. Melody spent three years in a wheelchair, underwent numerous surgeries and massive amounts of rehabilitation, and eventually was able to walk again, but with a pronounced limp.

After the accident, her mother suggested that she should join the Hemlock Society because they believe in suicide. Melody called a suicide hotline, and they said they'd never heard of a parent trying to talk their kid into suicide. She remembered a man that she met in a support program telling her, "Your mother is Hitler, your sister is Mussolini, and you're Poland."

The more I heard this woman's story, the more I understood why she presented herself as having survived more than many of us would have been physically capable of enduring. Fortunately, she'd developed several coping skills that helped her along the way. Her tremendous sense of humor was one of those skills; she said that if she hadn't been able to add humor to the telling of this story, she would've been unable to relate it and would've continued to keep it inside. She clearly presented herself as an extremely well-educated woman, even though she described school as a washout for her. I asked how she'd become so well read and well educated, and she replied, "Just on my own. You know, I'd read a lot." She also said that one of the reasons she had such a way with words was that she was always preparing for those two-against-one onslaughts from her mother and sister. "I had to learn to express myself," she said, "I always needed a quick answer."

During the rehabilitation process, when Melody was sick and helpless, her mother became friendlier, but the world did not. Following the coma, the wheelchair confinement, and the years of operations and rehabilitation, Melody experienced a lot of public humiliation. The same world that couldn't jump fast enough to light her cigarettes when she was gorgeous and living in Los Angeles ended up calling her names like "hop-along," "gimp," and "jester."

Unfortunately, her mother's turnaround was short-lived. Upon learning that Melody had collected a lot of money from a lawsuit, her mother changed again and told her that she should commit suicide so her nephew could inherit the money and go to college. Her mother thought it was sad that Melody had all the money.

By the time she finished telling her story that day at the Equine Experience, Melody appeared to have some relief. She'd looked extremely troubled when she arrived, but by the time we left the group area to walk into the arena and work with the horses, Melody seemed lighter. She was smiling a different sort of smile. It wasn't giddy or nervous, and her face seemed to be ringed in light. She'd forgotten about being thrown, and any other negative experience she'd had around horses. For the first time in 40 years, she walked right up to the horse without hesitation. Immediately, without waiting for the usual cue, he gave her his hoof. It seemed like the most natural thing in the world, almost as if he'd looked up and seen a kindred spirit, someone just as pure as he was. As the horse did everything she asked him to do, Melody laughed with delight.

By the time we got to the round pen where participants take turns working with one horse at liberty, Melody, who'd been the most withdrawn person I'd seen in many years at the Equine Experience, was the first to volunteer. She walked into the round pen with the whip in her hand, looked at the horse, and smiled. Rarely have I seen anyone communicate so clearly without using their body. Normally, the horse receives its cues from the person's body language. It knows whether to walk, trot, canter, gallop, or turn around and go the other way because the person indicates those commands by facing in the desired direction, turning the shoulders just so, standing at the correct angle. With Melody, the horse began to trot as she laughed playfully, then he began to canter. She just stood there without using any portion of her body. I'm not exaggerating when I say this: She really didn't move. From the sheer power of her spirit, she worked the horse at three different gaits and turned him in the opposite direction, simply by being so present.

It's hard for me to put into words what I see in my heart and mind as I remember Melody in that round pen. It's almost like writing the perfect love song—words are insufficient, but I'll never forget what happened that day. It was one of the most joyful times I've ever experienced in doing my work, and it was an inspiring example of someone using the five steps to walk through fear and self-doubt.

That day at Miraval, Melody acknowledged publicly for the first time that she'd been terrified all of her life. She quantified the fear at a level of nine out of a possible ten and admitted that she'd been living that way for many years. She talked about the worst-case scenario and figured that it had already happened, so she had nothing to lose by stepping out and trying. She sure had the willingness and the guts to do just that. She had the courage to confront her old fear of horses, walk on unsteady legs up to something that weighed about 1,700 pounds, and communicate with it using the power of her spirit and a body in which she was as uncomfortable as anyone I've ever seen.

By the time we finished working with the horse and got back to the group area to process what had gone on, Melody's fellow group members were looking at her almost in awe. The smile on her lips and the glow on her face was just the beginning of a celebration that has continued to this day.

Melody Revisited

One day, about a year and a half after she left Miraval, Melody called me from her car. She said she was looking at her reflection in a mirror, seeing herself more clearly than ever before. She knew she was different from the person she'd been for the last 50 years. She'd joined a gym and lost 40 pounds, but most important, she'd gotten tremendous relief by simply following the five-step process for dealing with the terror in her life.

As we talked on the phone, Melody told me that from 1988 until she came to Miraval, she'd walked with a pronounced limp, but that was no longer the case. She said, "I think it was a combination of going to Miraval and then going home and reading your book *It's Not about the Horse,* especially Vanessa's story."

Vanessa was a woman who'd been raped and left feeling like her body had been stolen from her. When Melody read what I told Vanessa—that her perpetrator or abuser didn't own her body—Melody knew that if someone like Vanessa could reclaim her body, then so could be she. She thought to herself, *I'm going to stop limping.*

"My life had gone down a lot further than most people's," Melody said. "It was like my body wasn't my own, but not because of being molested by the gas man. It was more the suspicions and the shame of being accused of things I'd never done by my family members than it had to do with being molested by a stranger."

As she read Vanessa's story, she said, "I was reading the book and I couldn't put it down, but I was afraid that the material was just too heavy and I kind of needed a breather."

She decided to walk across the street to get a soda, something she normally didn't do because she never walked anywhere unless she absolutely had to. That day, she made a conscious decision to take a short stroll.

She said, "I was walking down the street, and before crossing I had to go down about a block. All of a sudden in my left leg, I felt the hip joint pop. It dropped about three-quarters of an inch and then it felt kind of sore inside. I thought, *Oh my God! This is so phenomenal!*"

After 17 years of walking with her right foot and dragging the left, Melody was suddenly walking normally. The synchronicity of putting one foot in front of the other was incredible for her, and it happened because she first began by emotionally putting one foot in front of the other.

Melody couldn't wait to share the good news with her friends, including a trainer she'd been working with at the gym. When the trainer saw the way Melody was walking, she burst into tears. She couldn't believe her eyes. She'd tried so hard to help Melody with every kind of modern equipment and exercise she knew, but nothing had worked.

Melody continued, "When I went in there, it was like the glory of the coming of the Lord!" Everyone she knew was so excited for her. Her sister, her brother, and her brother's wife (a doctor) could hardly believe what had happened. Melody said, "I feel better. I look better. I feel like one of the living instead of the living dead."

I asked, "Melody, how much time do you spend during the day now being afraid?"

"Afraid?" she said, "Not much."

In just 18 months, Melody went from being 100 percent scared all the time to being unafraid 98 percent of the time. She feels as if miracles have occurred, and if this can happen, who knows what's next.

That day on the phone, she said, "I've lived very much in the past, but you know, today is wonderful. I'm on my way to Palm Springs with a friend of mine. It's a bright, beautiful day and we're in a Volvo, driving. So that's a wonderful day, don't you think so, Wyatt?" I had to agree that it was.

Melody's trip to Miraval was no accident. I think she'd been heading to a place of help for the longest time. The fact that she ended up reading a book that contained a story similar to her own just proves how important it is that we tell our stories, because those accounts can help others heal. Otherwise, we suffer the abuse in vain, and there is no justice. That never has been the case and won't be for as long as we're here, and as long as we're willing to share our experiences.

When I talked with Melody about including her story in this book, she was delighted but wondered why I'd want to write about someone who'd been scared 24 hours a day, seven days a week for 50 years. I told her it was because she's an absolute miracle! She told me that on the day we'd worked together at Miraval, her journey toward freedom had begun. She'd been living her life in chains, and it felt as if someone had taken them off. She felt a little sore underneath, but it was better than being in chains.

I'm so grateful to this brave woman for allowing me to use her story. The last thing I said to her I meant with all my heart. I told her, "I want you to know something. Meeting you has been one of the highlights of my work. I think you're absolutely delightful, and I'm grateful that you're willing to share this. Your story is going to be a huge inspiration to others, just like Vanessa's was to you."

She replied, "Oh God, I hope so. That would mean so much to me."

A Willing Participant

I hope that as you read this book, you understand that I don't see what I have to say as being "the solution" for everybody. I certainly don't have anyone's answers but my own. However, I do know that the journey itself is rewarding and that it can invoke change, sometimes in the most unexpected of ways.

As far back as I can remember, I've carried a fear of heights with me. It's called acrophobia, and I'm told that a lot of people who suffer from addictive disorders suffer from this, also. I certainly have it in spades. I have such a fear of heights that I have tremendous difficulty watching a trapeze act on television. If I were to go to the top of a tall building, I'd have to stand quite a distance away from the edge, and even that would feel tantamount to impending death. A 12-foot ladder frightens me. Being on the roof of a regular-size home terrifies me.

I remember living in Tennessee, in a single-story house. Some shingles had come loose, and I decided to fix them. As I got up on the roof, I must have looked like a chicken walking on a hot stove, every step cautiously chosen. I'm sure I looked like something in total slow motion, and I was absolutely terrified. I had to get down off the roof and hire somebody else to fix it. That experience caused me to feel all kinds of self-condemnation and, of course, I felt terrified at the same time. The fear and self-doubt literally chased me off the roof.

To document how these emotions play out in the human mind and body, I decided that, for the purposes of this book, I would attempt to overcome my fear of heights, exploring the emotions I felt during the process and utilizing the five steps. Documenting these emotions was really the second of two reasons for taking on this challenge. The first, of course, was to confront and walk through my fear of heights. As I said earlier, willingness is the key, so I decided to turn up the volume and see how it would translate onto paper.

This idea came about in part because of a man named Reid Tracy, the president and CEO of Hay House, Inc., the company that publishes my books. I was sitting in a hotel room in Scottsdale, Arizona, when Reid approached me about writing book number two. "What would it be about?" he asked.

As a spur-of-the-moment response, I said, "What to do when you don't know what to do by walking through fear and self-doubt."

"Perfect," Reid replied. "When are you going to start?"

"You know, I really don't know where to start."

"What's one of the biggest fears you've got?" he asked.

I described my fear of heights, and Reid, having some awareness of the programs at Miraval, asked me about some of the challenge activities that have heights associated with them. I told him about the Quantum Leap, an exercise in which participants climb a 30-foot pole. When they reach the top, they climb onto a little platform about the size of a pizza pan and stand up. Although they wear a safety harness, there's nothing to hold onto. For someone as terrified of heights as I am, this is no easy feat. I'd attempted it six years ago, but only got as far as eye level with the top of the pole before freezing, and being unable to take the last few steps up onto the platform.

Reid suggested, "Well, maybe that's where you need to start, and maybe that will get you off the dime so you can start writing." He looked at me and laughed, then said, "So get your ass up the pole and let's get this book done!"

As you'll see in the chapters that follow, that's exactly what I did.

≒✳≒

Chapter Three

Step 1: Acknowledge the Fear and Self-Doubt

It's almost midnight on April 16, 2003. I went to bed early tonight to get plenty of rest in preparation for tomorrow afternoon, when I'm going to do what I promised Reid Tracy and get my ass up that pole. I woke up approximately 30 minutes ago with my head racing and realized that the pole is not the issue.

I think what I'm about to confront has nothing to do with anything other than my own belief system about myself: what I should be, what I'm not, what others are going to see, what I'm going to be forced to look at. The stories going on in my head are endless.

On a daily basis, I'm able to sit with people, comfort them, and be supportive and understanding so that they might walk through their own fear and self-doubt. Now it's my turn once again.

I didn't realize how difficult this was going to be or how it was going to manifest itself. Intellectually, I know that I can strap into the safety harness and feel physically safe as I climb the 30-foot pole. I've done that part before, but I couldn't take the last step. I didn't even try. Instead, I went through the pretense of saying, "At least I went as far as I could, and that's okay."

Those words were nothing more than a form of mental masturbation. I had to make myself believe it was okay. If I'd tried to take that last step, I would've been forced to confront what I'm about to get in touch with tomorrow. I'm not even sure what that is or what I'm feeling right now, but I think it's about admitting the physical limitations (or the perceived physical limitations) of a 60-year-old man who hasn't taken care of his body.

I remember playing baseball in college and being able to stay behind the plate as catcher for an entire game, bouncing up and down on my knees for nine long innings. My legs were extremely strong then, but today I have so much pain in my legs and knees that I can't squat down anymore. I've lost all the cartilage between the two main bones in my legs at the knee joints. People often ask me what's wrong as they watch me walk with an unconscious favoring of whichever leg hurts the most that day.

Basically, this comes down to a fear that if people see who I really am, they'll feel sorry for me. I really would feel ashamed if that happened. I tell people on a daily basis that it's okay to be afraid and it's okay to doubt themselves. I tell them that we've been programmed to doubt ourselves. Yet it's not okay for me right now.

If this sounds melodramatic, it isn't. This shit is real. It's been there forever. I just don't want to avoid it anymore. I notice how naturally the anger comes up to deal with it, and I try to offset it. I want to be able to walk through this without raging at it. I want to tap in to the depths of what it means to walk through this stuff at a deeper level than I've heretofore attempted.

Agreeing to write this book has presented me with this opportunity. If I can't walk through this experience, record it, and share it with anybody who's willing to open up the pages, it's as if there's no integrity in my work.

If I hadn't come in here and sat down and begun to write about this, I'm afraid I would've spent a sleepless night. It's now approximately 12:30 A.M., which means it's the day of the climb, and it seems less threatening now than it did an hour ago when I woke up.

I woke up feeling lonely, but I'm not alone. I woke up doubting myself at levels that have nothing to do with present-moment time. This experience is bringing up all the trauma and all the beliefs that I've had about who I should be as opposed to who I am. This all has to be confronted today. I'm sure there are those who will read this and ask, "What the hell are you doing this for? Look at the things you've overcome." I haven't overcome anything 100 percent, nothing, except maybe my willingness to look at what's scary and to look at my shame.

This shame business is really some dark stuff. It feels like I'm walking through goo of some kind. It smells bad. It feels bad. It's cold and hot at the same time. It feels like I'm close to the core of what my problems have been for much of my life. I don't know whether I'll be able to stand up on the pole or not. I don't know if my legs will support me or not, and I'm going to have to deal with

*what's left. After that, it just doesn't seem quite
as big as it did when I first woke up tonight.*

How Do We Know When We're Afraid?

In the first chapter, we defined fear and self-doubt, explored what causes it, and talked about the consequences of letting these emotions continue unchecked. Now it's time to examine some of the symptoms. We can't acknowledge our fear if we don't recognize it, so how do we know when we're afraid? What does it feel like? How do we act?

As you probably noticed from my pre-climb notes, one of the things that I do as a man—because I've been conditioned to respond to my fear by getting angry—is to start with the anger and trace it backwards. Finding out where the fear originated, what set it off, is one way to recognize it, but there are physical and emotional clues as well. If these clues were acknowledged early in life, when we were children, we wouldn't have to use defense mechanisms such as anger or busying ourselves with compulsive behaviors in order to deal with our fear and self-doubt. We could just say, "This is what it is, and it's okay to be afraid because that happens to people." In a healthy culture that honors the body, we wouldn't miss these clues, and we could learn to deal with fear and self-doubt in a healthy way.

Listening to the Body

It's so important to pay attention to our bodies, but in our culture we're pretty much taught to dislike them. We're always comparing ourselves to people who have the "perfect bodies," few of whom we ever see walking up and down the streets of the major cities of America or anyplace else. Because we're not comfortable in our bodies, we spend a lot of time not paying any attention to them internally. In other words, we miss or ignore the clues they provide.

Did you know that much of the machinery on this planet is designed along the lines of the human body? Ever hear of cars that have ball-joint suspensions? Where was the original ball joint? In the human hip. Headlights, where are they? On the front of that automobile, just as our eyes are on the front of our heads. They aren't on the side. What's a fuel pump? It's the heart of an engine. Just as we've got to have water in us, so does an engine. Just as we need synovial fluid to lubricate our joints, an engine needs things like motor oil and transmission fluid. It's actually safer to be a car in this culture than it is to be a human, because cars get more attention. We know how to fix those machines. We pay attention when there's a knock in a car, but we ignore the knocks in our bodies.

Our bodies carry all of our unsolved mysteries, all of our unhealed wounds that have been covered with scar tissue. Our bodies tap us on the shoulder all the time, saying, "Now's the time. Maybe now's the time." That's one of the reasons we feel uncomfortable in our bodies, because we're constantly getting these messages but we try so hard to ignore them. We've never been taught that it's okay to heal. That's what this is about: healing.

People in our culture often say things like, "You should be over that by now." How can you be over something if you've never dealt with it? That's like telling a flat tire that it shouldn't have gone flat. Yes, it should have, if it had worn down to where the tread was gone and the steel showed through. It probably gave plenty of warnings—there were knots on the tire the whole time—but the owner ignored them until the tire finally went flat.

The same thing can happen to us. We get all these opportunities to replace our old tires with new ones, we get chances to patch or repair them, but we don't do it. If we ignore the signs long enough, we'll eventually become totally nonfunctional. We have the responsibility to decide which outcome will occur.

Tuning In to Our Own Clues

If I want to know if I'm afraid, I have to tune in to my particular clues. It can help if you tell me about your clues, but I need to know how mine feel. For example, I know I'm afraid when my heart starts to beat fast, combined with blood rushing to my ears. A huge threat feels as if a large hoofed animal has stepped right in the pit of my stomach. It almost takes my breath away, and it feels very restrictive. Feeling hopeless and feeling fearful are the same things for me. Feeling the need to exit a situation immediately, before I've even given it a chance to unfold, is an immediate trigger for me that fear is present. The fact that I'm making up stories to defend myself is another clue that tells me I'm afraid. When I'm making up stories about other people—trying to anticipate their opening remarks and preparing my response—it usually means I'm feeling defensive or just plain scared. Those are the physical ways my body tells me that I'm in fear.

Quite often, when I'm attempting to discover whether fear is present, I'll ask myself, "How old do I feel right now?" If the answer is less than my current age, that tells me there's something going on that needs my attention. Maybe I've had a charge about something and need to talk to someone about it or get a reality check about it, see where it comes from, and try to heal it.

I know some people who go numb. This type of fear is usually trauma based. People who've experienced either physical or emotional trauma, and haven't worked through it, will go absolutely numb if anything in the present reminds them of the past. You can't touch them with a harsh word or even with physical pain, because they don't hear you. They've shut their system down because of their absolute terror about what might happen next.

Rage is another symptom of fear, and men are famous for raging. Shame- and fear-based men are ragers, and a scared man can be a dangerous man. A normal anger response isn't dangerous, because it's not fueled by years and years of repressed anger—it's just something that happens in the moment, it's expressed, and it goes away. But a scared man can be dangerous because he's wondering whether he's going to survive. Our basic drive in life is to stay alive, and when we feel as if our very lives are in danger, we'll do just about anything to protect ourselves. I look at people like Mike Tyson. He must be terrified because he's a dangerous man. I watch how he defends himself with words and how he shocks people with his conversation, and I sometimes look at him and feel very sad. I wonder what it was like for him as a little boy and how he must have been treated to be exhibiting that level of viciousness at this point in time. There has to be a lot of pain under all that. It's all logical, but it's still scary.

Men are especially dangerous because they've been conditioned to believe that feeling fear is not okay, it's a shameful thing, but a scared woman can be dangerous, too. Women are given more permission to experience their feelings, so when they're afraid they're usually able to feel it, and they aren't as terrified as most men are.

No matter what sex we are, or how old, or any other factor we can dream up, it's important to take that first step and acknowledge the fear. When it's kept secret, it's like a gland condition that continues to cook. As soon as it's acknowledged, it loses some of its power.

Strange but True: External Clues

Approximately six months prior to the incident with my heart that I described in the Preface of this book, my car would quite often lose power. It appeared to be getting too much gas or maybe not enough. It would choke down to the point of stalling, and then be able to start again. I'd taken it to the dealership on a couple of occasions, but the mechanics there couldn't find anything wrong. I took it to an import mechanic who connected it to his computerized diagnostic machines, but he couldn't seem to find the problem either. The problem recurred, so I took the car to an import auto-service center. The mechanic there said, "The only thing I can figure is that you have a plaque buildup within the engine. I'm going to give you a chemical to clean that out, and the car should run fine." We put the additive in the engine and, sure enough, no more problems.

Isn't it ironic that, prior to my experiencing a near heart attack (which I didn't have), similar symptoms were manifesting themselves in my physical possessions? Coincidence? Well, no, I don't think so. I happen to believe that physical possessions such as our homes and automobiles are extensions or expressions of ourselves.

Whatever your belief system concerning something like this, my opinion is that paying attention to everything that goes on in our immediate world can certainly be beneficial, as opposed to ignoring it, as we've been conditioned and accustomed to doing. It seems as if our souls are in continuous contact and cooperation with the universe we live in. If we pay attention to the way they interact, our lives can certainly be lived in a more conscious and joyous way.

If anything like this ever occurs again, you'd better believe that I will at least pay a visit to the doctor to see if something internal is manifesting itself externally.

Being Impeccable with Our Word

A couple of years ago, I was privileged to sit in the audience and listen to Don Miguel Ruiz, the author of *The Four Agreements,* when he came to speak in Tucson. One of the things that struck me most about his lecture was when he told us about leaving his culture and going out into the world.

Don Miguel was raised in the Toltec tradition in Mexico, where his grandfather was a tribal elder and a Toltec shaman. He was viewed as a holy man, a great teacher, and a person of knowledge. When

Don Miguel left home to pursue his formal education, he rejected the teachings that he'd been exposed to growing up. He became seduced instead by the world culture, was educated as a medical doctor, and returned home with the primary intention of using his newfound knowledge to confront his grandfather's Toltec beliefs. As the story goes, his grandfather granted him an audience and listened patiently to him for about an hour and a half to two hours. As Don Miguel concluded his dissertation about the primitive nature of the Toltec beliefs, he looked at his grandfather and said, "So, what do you think?"

His grandfather looked him straight in the eyes and said to him, "Lies, all lies," and then proceeded to tell him why. At that point in time, Don Miguel began his "graduate study" of his own culture and later became a Toltec master himself.

As I went about my work the next day, the people who work with me asked if I remembered anything about the lecture. Was it any good? What had I learned? For the next hour and a half, I pretty much told them verbatim what Don Miguel Ruiz had said. I've never been able to do such a thing before or since, and I certainly don't have a photographic memory. But I'd been completely open to this man who had great power and who'd gone through a journey that had brought him to a place of truth. He was a superb communicator. He spoke broken English, but it was almost as if everything he said bypassed any type of filter system that I had and was imprinted within my psyche. I was very impressed and continue to be to this day.

One of the things that he spoke about was being impeccable with our word. He stressed repeatedly that the most important thing for us to watch in regard to our conversation is not so much what we say to others, but what we say to ourselves. I'm totally convinced that this is of paramount importance, because what we tell ourselves is primarily what we'll be saying to others on a daily basis. We must pay attention to our own stories and how we repeat them to ourselves moment to moment as we live our lives.

This is the only way to live a life of integrity—to not only question what is said to us, but to scrutinize what we say to ourselves and to others. The process of walking through self-doubt and fear will create the opportunity and the necessity to pay close attention to the words we repeat to ourselves. Before we can influence any of the systems in which we participate, walk through, touch, or interact with, we first must have integrity in the system that we carry within the confines of our own human skin, and that's a system of energy.

I often say that our bodies are made up of approximately three dollars' worth of minerals, with the remainder being water held together by skin. The water conducts the electricity of who we are. We are a force, and until we take responsibility for that, we'll continue to be led by the systems of the world; be influenced by them; and be lied to, seduced, and fooled by them. To blame the systems certainly isn't the way for us to take responsibility for the fact that we're in them and helped create them. We can't change another system, and we don't have the right to do so, but we do have the obligation and the right to change the system and the energy that each of us calls "me"—especially if that system doesn't work.

If some of the information and some of the programming that we've taken on don't work in ways that bring joy into our lives, we're obligated to change that. Each of us should be a walking, breathing example of the joy of living. The only way that I know to do that is to walk through the fear and self-doubt that we've adopted over the years as a pattern of survival. As we walk through it, we change "surviving" to "living." As Don Miguel says, we must be impeccable with our word. When we feel fear, we must acknowledge it. When we feel self-doubt, we must acknowledge it. What we say to ourselves is the most important conversation, and it goes on all day.

Jack's Story

I first met Jack at a conference in November 2002 in Scottsdale, Arizona. This 64-year-old recovering alcoholic who had been clean and sober for 12 years introduced himself to me after attending a workshop I'd just given. He told me that he'd transitioned from chemical addiction and alcoholism to workaholism, which ultimately made him an extremely wealthy man. He also stated that his job was his identity, and that achieving tasks had been his way of hoping to change his sense of self-worth since the age of nine. He said he'd felt "a deep connection" to me, and he sensed that if we could spend some time together, he could get some help with his severe bouts of depression.

In the spring of 2003, Jack came to a three-and-a-half-day intensive workshop I facilitated at Miraval. It featured work with the horses in the morning, and three hours of group forum work in the afternoon, for a total of six hours a day. When he arrived at the workshop, Jack was a physical and emotional wreck. He was extremely depressed and terrified, and he suffered from periodontal disease and two legs that wouldn't support him. On the first night, when we began by introducing ourselves, he immediately became tearful, and his voice was extremely shaky, as was his physical body.

The next morning, during our first day of experiential work at the Equine Experience, Jack stated that he was about to enter into retirement and had no idea what he'd be able to do with himself, since his entire identity was tied up in his work. When he walked into the arena to work with the horses, he immediately began to sob and was in a childlike state.

During our interaction that day, Jack was able to process a lot of his fear and gain some relief by acknowledging in public for the first time just what his basic concerns were. Later that morning, as one of the women in the group worked with her horse, she asked Jack to come into the arena to be of emotional support to her. Jack was sitting on a crate, and his body was so shaky and his legs were so weak that two people had to help him up. His body was so saturated with fear that it was literally taking away the power of his muscles and skeletal system. It was one of the deepest manifestations of fear invading a person's body and robbing first his spirit and then his physical being that I had ever encountered in my 23-year career.

On the second day of the workshop, Jack seemed to be a little more at ease but still extremely tearful. When we were checking in for the afternoon group-forum session, he burst into tears and said,

"I totally need to work this afternoon. I'm terrified once again, and I'm feeling helpless." Despite the superior achievements in his career, he appeared to have few coping skills for handling his fear and pain.

I asked Jack to step into the middle of the room and sit down on a throw pillow that I'd placed on the floor. I joined him in the middle of the room and asked him to tell the entire group his life story. The experience he described was nothing less than horrible.

Jack's father was an alcoholic, and his parents divorced when he was five years old. The next year, his mother committed suicide and Jack was the one who found her. Until he was 53 years old, Jack was unwilling to acknowledge his mother's suicide and had completely repressed the cause of her death. He went immediately into denial and just told the story that his mother had passed away. He'd kept the memory repressed with chemicals and work for all those years.

His father had signed custody over to Jack's paternal grandparents, a scenario that turned out to be disastrous. Jack's grandparents abused him physically and verbally throughout his entire time with them. When he was only nine years old, his grandmother told him that his father had given him away with the understanding that they would never give him back. His grandmother also told him that he'd never amount to anything because he was his father's son.

Jack told us about his five marriages, the fifth of which had lasted the longest and continued to be his most successful to date. He told us that he was happy with his present wife, and that they had entered into recovery together. His second and third wives had both told him the same thing that his grandmother had, that he'd never amount to anything. Each time he heard those words, he'd suck up a big breath inside and think, *God dammit, you watch! You'll see.* With his rage and his drive to prove them wrong, he went on to become a very rich man.

As we spoke that afternoon, I observed that Jack appeared to be in a childlike state. When I asked him how old he felt, he immediately went to nine years of age. It didn't take long to discover that Jack had been stuck in a nine-year-old traumatized emotional state for most of his adult life. Although he'd gone through four marriages in an adult man's body, he'd done it with the emotional coping skills of a nine-year-old boy. When I asked him if this was possible, he immediately agreed that he'd never known how to be a husband, and he had no idea what he was doing.

As Jack worked on separating the traumatized nine-year-old child from the man sitting on the cushion on the floor in 2003, he was able to access his own spiritual awareness, and answers that created a safe place internally. With his eyes closed, he used his breath to bring himself into present-moment time, without losing sight of the wounded and devastated nine-year-old boy. Jack had finally become the parent he'd never had—a healthy, nurturing, understanding father. He was able to relieve the nine-year-old of being responsible for anything other than being taken care of by Jack, the soon-to-be-retired adult. He acknowledged the pain that this child had gone through all of his life and was finally able to say, "I now know what to do with my retirement years. I'm going to become the parent to myself that I never experienced."

As Jack concluded his work, I looked around the room and noticed that everyone was in tears, expressing huge amounts of compassion for Jack as he sat there on the floor. I also noticed that Jack's face had grown softer, and his brow was not nearly as furrowed. He was visibly calmer and more at peace.

I knew intuitively what was about to happen. Keep in mind that during the previous morning's work, Jack had needed assistance to get up off the crate and walk into the arena to help a fellow participant. During this afternoon session, I looked at him and said, "What I'd like you to do now is stand up." Jack sprang to his feet! There was a gasp from the entire room, accompanied by cheers and applause. Jack looked totally surprised. His tears were replaced by a beaming smile. I was in tears, too. It was a moment of total elation for us all.

Throughout the remainder of the workshop, Jack would spontaneously say, "I need a moment!" He'd spring to his feet and throw his hands up like a circus performer. What a gift! This was such a manifestation of the spiritual power of a man who'd given meaning to his pain. He'd corrected a huge misperception about himself and discovered the self-worth that he hadn't known he'd possessed all along.

As I spoke with him two weeks later, Jack told me that his condition was still improving. He and his wife were continuing the celebration.

Occurrences like this are the reason I enjoy being here. It was wonderful and gratifying to watch Jack walk through not just fear, but absolute terror, and come out on the other side where he learned that there was nothing wrong with him as a human being, and his fear was no longer in charge of his life. It also gave me the opportunity to witness the miracle of the human spirit, and to realize that acknowledging our fears is the first step in making miracles happen.

The Journey Begins with a Single Step

If I had a dollar for every time I've made up a story about someone so as to prepare myself for what I was afraid might be the inevitable, the possibility of my getting hurt, I could be retired by now. I'd be a rich man. I've spent much of my life making up stories. If you've read this far, you've probably become very clear about that in regard to my behavior.

In the early 1990s, I was working for the company I still work for, but in a different capacity. I was in an executive position and was informed that there was a restructuring taking place within the company and that my new boss would be a lady named Judy McCaleb.

Now, Judy was one of those people whom I'd made up a story about. She was extremely intelligent, attractive, well put together in appearance, very matter-of-fact in her approach, and from my point of view, something of an "ice queen," whatever that means. I surmised that she'd risen to the height of her career not by being the nurturing kind of female that I enjoy being around, but by being someone with a couple of steel rods down her back. She was sharp, ruthless (in my opinion), and a no-nonsense type of person—in other words, a very powerful, self-assured woman.

Upon learning that Judy was going to be my new boss, I was immediately triggered into feeling like a helpless little boy, even though I was in my mid-40s, stood 6'4", and weighed about 220 pounds at the time. In and of itself, my assessment of Judy as an "ice queen" was the foundation for my fear, and had I continued to foster it, I'm sure it would have prevented us from ever having a productive relationship. Luckily, I'd been taught about the five steps for overcoming fear and self-doubt.

I knew that if I didn't become proactive with my fear, I wouldn't enjoy coming to work the next day. Rather than letting that happen, I called Judy immediately and made an appointment to meet with her the following afternoon.

The next day, when I walked into her office, she was sitting behind her desk in what I refer to as a power suit, emitting enough energy to light up Delaware. Looking up at me, she asked, "What can I do for you, Wyatt?"

I said, "When I found out yesterday that you were going to be my new boss, I immediately became uncomfortable."

She looked at me and asked, "Why?"

I replied, "I'm afraid of you."

Her face immediately softened, and she looked puzzled as she asked me, "Why is that, do you think?"

I remember telling her, "It's not about you. It has to do with my not knowing how to deal with powerful women, and it's an old thing. I'm in therapy, as you well know, and I'm continuing to work on everything that scares me. This just happens to be a stop-off along the way."

She smiled, her eyes softening again, as she said, "I so appreciate you, and I've been looking forward to the opportunity of working with you."

This came as a total surprise to me. She went on to tell me how much she admired many of my attributes, including my sensitivity, my kindness, and my straightforward approach to my work and how I live my life. She added, "One of the reasons I've looked forward to working with you is that I know you're trustworthy, because you walk your talk."

That day, I began a really wonderful relationship with a truly amazing human being.

Much later, I found out that Judy had presented herself professionally as a powerful and straightforward woman in order to keep her own boundaries intact. She wanted to be acknowledged as being as powerful as the rest of the type A personalities in the office with her—namely, the men. She certainly held her own in any meeting I ever attended. She also brought a lot of heart to a situation, which anyone who worked with her could have learned from.

We worked together for a period of months before Judy decided to resign from her position and move on to a full partnership with her husband in a successful development business here in Tucson. The day she announced her decision to leave the company was one of the most powerful events that I've witnessed in any type of executive meeting. As I said before, my original perception was totally erroneous. Judy was extremely well loved and well thought of, and when she announced her plans to leave, half of the grown men in the room were in tears.

Over the years, which number about 13 now, I haven't lost touch with Judy. She's one of the kindest, sweetest souls I've ever met. She continues to be totally successful in her life and has shown up here at Miraval on two or three occasions with friends. As a fellow spiritual traveler, she continues her journey, part of which has included participating in, and working with me in, the Equine Experience.

I recently asked her if I could write about her in this second book, and she was deeply touched. Just about every time I see her, we wind up misty-eyed, remembering that day when I walked in and did my best to clear my stuff out of the way so that I could let her into my heart. Her stuff wasn't in her way; she was already prepared to let me in. It was my issue, as is often the case.

I'm constantly given opportunities to use these wonderful tools that were given to me years ago, which I've been able to work with, develop, and add to over the years to make my life so much richer. What has always and will continue to make my life the most fertile of landscapes for spiritual and emotional growth is my willingness to acknowledge and quantify my fear, to look at the worst-case scenario, to get information that's supportive, walk through the fear, and come out on the other side with a smile on my face. That first step is the most important. It all starts with acknowledging the problem, and the problem is usually fear and self-doubt.

Thank you, Judy, for allowing me to use this example in these writings, and thank you most of all for being my friend.

⊯✳⊯

Chapter Four

Step 2: Quantify the Fear and Self-Doubt

I lay in bed tonight and rehearsed scenario after scenario of what might happen, and in the process, I went through a maze of self-doubt and fear. I looked at my physical limitations, not wanting to look at just how severe they've become over the years. In addition to the pain in my knees, I've got two bad shoulders, so there's a possibility for some fairly serious pain, which I know I can live through physically. There's no doubt in my mind about that; I just don't look forward to it. I feel the emotional pain so much more.

I've begun to quantify the fear, which from moment to moment varies. It goes all the way from doubting myself emotionally and spiritually, to questioning my own worth as a human being, certainly my worth as a man. If you ask me to quantify how much is there, at times it's beyond a ten. Most of the time that I've lain awake and thought about it, it's been in the area of between five and eight, probably because my head takes over at times and rationalizes.

I'm going back to bed now so that I might sleep, so that maybe tomorrow won't be as challenging as it could have been had I not gotten enough rest. I feel embarrassed writing about this at this point in time. As I sit here and write about feeling embarrassed, I automatically feel pissed off. Sitting here alone in the second bedroom in our home, I'm pissed because I've chosen to climb a 30-foot pole tomorrow. What a crazy zoo life is sometimes . . . and yet it isn't.

What's in a Name?

When it comes to fear and self-doubt, we must be willing to acknowledge their existence before we can take the next steps and deal with them. For many of us, particularly men, acknowledging the fear is not always easy because we've been taught in our culture to minimize everything we feel. We've grown up watching football players on the field as they take a brutal hit, then slowly get back on their feet and say, "No big deal." We've seen male role models who fall down and break an arm, then stand up and say, "It's not that bad. I'm fine." We've heard parents tell their little boys, "Don't be such a baby. Big boys don't cry."

In order for a man to acknowledge fear, he quite often has to be at the point of getting ready to do battle or tear something up or scream or throw something, when in fact he's been angry for days prior to that. Most men don't even want to use the word *anger,* let alone the word *fear.* We'd rather call it "being a little frustrated" or "feeling a little irritated."

It doesn't make any sense to me that we have eight or ten words to describe one emotion. If we picked up a key to a car and someone asked what it was, we'd say, "It's a key." But if we used the same system to describe a key that we use to describe our emotions, we might call that key an opening device, an entry-level instrument, an igniting tool—anything but what it really is. It's a friggin' key!

Listen, fear is fear, anger is anger, and shame is shame. If we're going to identify how much fear we have, let's start by calling it what it is. Let's not say, "I'm a little nervous" or "I'm feeling some trepidation." Let's just admit, "I'm scared, okay? I'm scared."

Take Back Your Power

When we call it what it is, we're forced to take the next step and ask ourselves, "How much fear is going on in my body?" As you may have noticed in some of the stories so far, when it comes to quantifying the fear, I recommend giving it a number from one to ten.

Now, if we've been trained to be self-critical, we won't want to acknowledge that we're feeling a seven or an eight. Oh my God, what would people think? That we're wimps, we have no social skills, we shouldn't be in the position we're in? That we probably shouldn't have lived this long and probably don't deserve to be here? That we've fooled them so far, but when they find out, they'll probably get rid of us.

Chances are they'd think, *I understand that!* You see, all those things that we believe other people will think are just stories we've made up in our heads. I've heard these stories laid out time after time, and that's exactly how ridiculous they can get.

It's so imperative to quantify the fear. When we simply admit, "This much is present," it takes out some of the starch and makes it seem manageable. When it's not as big as Mt. Kilimanjaro, we can hold it in our hands and deal with it.

How Bad Is Bad?

Just as it's important not to underestimate fear and self-doubt, it's equally important not to over-estimate these feelings or give them more power than they deserve. If you're experiencing a fear level of ten, it means you believe that you may not survive. You're on overload and you don't think you can make it. However, just because it *feels* like a life-threatening ten doesn't mean your life really is in danger.

Unless you can look in front of you and see a man-eating predator, or someone holding a gun to your head, or signs that the nuke sirens have gone off, or symptoms that you're having a massive heart attack (have you lost feeling in an entire side of your body?), chances are that what you're calling a ten is not about what's going on right now. It simply means that what's going on right now reminds you of, or is bringing up, something that you haven't dealt with, something that scared you when you were little.

If you could take one big breath and ask, "Is there a man-eating tiger in front of me? Is someone hold-ing a gun on me? Is this true?" you'd realize that you were simply on overload. Your fear is out of propor-tion to the current event. It's much like cranking up the volume on a sound system. In a high-quality system, the speakers can handle it. In an inferior system, the speakers blow out.

Giving yourself a reality check. Asking questions about what's really going on will help you step out of the fear and into present-moment time. Skip this step and you'll find yourself in overload, experiencing an anxiety attack, hyperventilating, breathing into a brown paper bag, and feeling defective.

How many times in your life have you thought you were going to die and you didn't? If you were to sit down and make a list, how many times have you said to yourself, "I may not make it through this"? Well, you made it through! The proof is that you're here, reading this book. The only reason you're feeling the fear again is because you haven't dealt with it yet. Overload is simply your body's way of trying to tell you, "You've held this in for a long time. Listen up; you're not going to die here. You've just been given a chance to deal with this thing."

Overload indicates a wound that needs to be healed, which means it's an opportunity. A lot of times, a fear level of ten is just a huge opportunity for your spirit to say, "It's time to heal this. We've postponed this long enough. Let's enhance the quality of our life. Let's get this out of the way so the energy doesn't burn up everything in sight."

We don't have to feel this way over and over again. All it takes to end the cycle is our willingness to address the situation. Every day, we wake up with the ability to ask ourselves, "How do I want life to be today? What am I going to do about it?" Willingness interrupts the cycle and lets us heal. Life will still go around and come around, but just like that tire we talked about earlier, it doesn't have to have a knot on it this time. It can roll along more smoothly when we quantify the fear and take the steps toward healing.

Paula's Story

One of the fears that I find present in the general population results from the trauma of having been favored by one parent or the other during the childhood years. A woman named Paula was such a person.

When Paula came to the Equine Experience, she was paired with a big thoroughbred horse named Vern. He wasn't cooperating with her at all, but she continued to reward him by petting him over and over again. I explained that she was rewarding the horse for his uncooperative behavior, and I suggested that she should stop petting him, but she might as well have been deaf for all the good it did. She just looked at me in a trancelike state, which is not unusual for someone in a relationship with any living thing.

Finally, Paula asked me directly for help. When I went over to her, her main question was: "What can I do that will cause this horse to lift his foot?" It was obviously a cerebral question. She was looking for a technique. Am I squeezing in the right place? Can you show me how hard to squeeze? I told her that there was no magic spot on a horse, and that there never has been. I asked her what she was feeling, because that's usually the biggest impediment. Her lip began to quiver and her eyes filled with tears. A minute elapsed, and she still wasn't able to answer, so I repeated the question. I asked her to please tell me what she was feeling and asked if it felt familiar to her.

"Yes," she replied.

"How long have you been feeling this?" I asked.

"Much of my life," she said, "since around the age of ten."

A few moments later, Paula was able to identify the feeling as loneliness. I continued to ask my usual set of questions regarding parental relationships, but Paula said that her lonely feelings pertained mainly to her siblings who had rejected her because she was favored in the family by both of their parents. Paula was a high achiever, very bright, quite open emotionally, and spontaneous, and both of her parents seemed to dote on her. This had not occurred with any of her older siblings; consequently, they resented her and treated her poorly.

When Vern refused to cooperate, Paula suddenly experienced the trauma of being rejected by her siblings. She said that whenever someone didn't cooperate with her, she felt devastated. She'd never realized that her feelings stemmed from a fear of rejection.

At this point, we were approximately 40 minutes into the experience, and Vern hadn't lifted one hoof off the ground. It was time to utilize the five steps to deal with Paula's fear and self-doubt.

She'd already acknowledged her fear of rejection, so next I asked her to quantify it. Her fear level on a scale of one to ten was an eight. Her worst-case scenario was that the horse would never cooperate, and that would mean she was a bad person. When she said that, I could see that she had the coping skills of a child, even though she was probably 40 years old. I asked if she'd been willing to sacrifice herself so that people would not reject her, and more tears came. She admitted that this was something she'd been doing most of her life, and it was very painful.

I asked Paula if she was willing to become internally focused and see herself as someone who deserved to have the people she was in a relationship with allow her to be herself and to shake her hand. When she was willing to do that, she walked up to Vern, and he immediately gave her his hoof.

She looked at me and asked, "How did that happen?"

She was in such a trance that she couldn't process the information. I had her put the hoof down, and we reprocessed everything, starting with the hoof and going backwards. She was then able to understand how she had sabotaged herself most of her life due to her terror of being rejected. This is a common occurrence with a lot of high-achieving people in family systems that don't know how to validate each other just for *being* rather than for performing a task well.

I asked her to go back to the horse, and she was immediately able to gain access to the remaining hooves. There was nothing to it. She almost felt guilty about her success, which gave her an indication of where the work needed to go from there.

In effect, Paula was apologizing for who she was, because being herself hadn't created the ideal circumstance in her family system. She'd uncovered an old wound that she'd reexperienced so many times that it had become part of her psyche. For the first time, she realized that she'd spent most of her life re-creating that family system—in her work relationships, her friendships, and her present-day family.

When the exercise was over, Paula talked about how much relief she felt. She promised to continue paying attention to what she was feeling and to try her best not to hide from her feelings from now on.

One of the things that will be imperative for her future development in dealing with her fear and self-doubt is to give herself permission to move on to Step 5 and celebrate the fact that she's gone through the first four steps. Her feelings of guilt about the relief she felt indicate how much healing needs to take place.

Until we're able to celebrate the fact that we've grown and walked through something that's been a lifetime impediment, we won't be able to give ourselves permission to do it again. If we don't believe we deserve to celebrate, chances are that we'll find a way to sabotage ourselves so we can continue in what's familiar, which is a painful, scary place.

One More Word about Willingness

Sometimes, when a problem seems insurmountable and we think it's a seven, eight, nine, or ten, our fear keeps us immobilized and we won't even take the first step toward overcoming it. This happens to all of us, again and again, but the more we practice, the easier it becomes.

As I began working on this book, I found myself stuck. I'd gotten about a third of it written, but didn't know what to do or say next. I started thinking, *I've already taken the money and used it. I'll need to go sell something to pay the publisher back, because I don't know if I can deliver this book. How the hell do I say these things?*

In the midst of all this, Carin commented that I seemed troubled. I admitted, "I'm afraid that I can't do this."

She asked, "How afraid are you?"

"It's about a nine or a ten, or maybe even worse. I'm afraid I'm just a one-story guy, and I really don't have anything else to say," I answered.

"Okay," she said. "What's the worst thing that could happen?"

"I guess I could give them the money back and say I just can't do it."

"Well, you could handle doing that, couldn't you?"

After thinking it over for a few seconds, I said, "Well, I guess I could. I lived almost 60 years without writing a book. I can live the next 60 without writing another one."

"Okay," Carin continued. "How could you get some information about how to really make this decision?"

"You know something," I remembered, "I haven't even talked to this editor they assigned." I'd met Gail briefly at the beginning of the project, but hadn't contacted her since. I said, "She seemed very smart, but I don't know."

You see, I'd made up another one of those stories in my head about this person, and I was letting it stop me from taking those first steps. Gail was assigned to me early in the project. From what I'd been told about her, I decided that she was a very high-powered person who'd had a couple of careers and is so bright that she sits around and just puts these books together. I figured that when I handed her something, I wanted it to be pretty much complete. I didn't want her to be bored or think that she'd picked up some idiot's ramblings here. All those things went through my head, and they were just more of the stories I'd made up, based on years and years of wondering if I'm okay.

After talking to Carin and walking through the first three steps (acknowledging the fear, quantifying it, and imagining the worst-case scenario), it was time to forget about the story I'd made up and do as she suggested: gather information and support. I e-mailed

Gail and told her I was stuck. Her response came right away: "Send me what you have and I'll offer some suggestions." I did what she asked, and everything just took off from there. As I assembled the pieces I'd written so far, I realized that I'd done more than I thought I had, which is often the case. Without going a single step further, I felt better already. I'd walked through the first three steps with Carin, I'd discovered a source of information and support, and with just a little bit of feedback, I was off and running again. Talk about taking that fifth step and celebrating!

The next day, I called my friend Danny Levin, who's in the sales area at Hay House. I told him, "Man, I'm feeling good today!"

"Why's that?" he asked.

"I'm unstuck," I explained. "I talked to Gail Fink today."

He said, "Wyatt, that's what editors are for."

There I was, just sitting around drop-kicking myself in the ass and wondering how many more times I was going to have go through this. I don't know the answer to that question, but I do know that I began to trust the process a little more. I have to add that the timing was amazing. It seems like universal perfection that I got mired in my own stuff and had to use the steps just when I was writing about them.

Because of my own fear and self-doubt, I hadn't used the resources that were so readily available to me. All I had to do was have a little faith, confront the story I'd made up, and take that first step on the hero's journey. No matter what path in life we're on—whether we want to write a book, swim a river, climb a mountain, or jump out of an airplane—chances are we'll have the opportunity to fight our own misperceptions about how capable we are. If we're willing to do that, we'll complete the hero's journey every day, in every act in which we participate. The worst-case scenario is that whatever we suspect about ourselves might really be true, that we're a piece of garbage, but I've never seen that play out for anyone.

Every time we confront our perceptions, we come up with a pearl. We expect to find something funky, but we usually discover a prize. It doesn't happen by chance, though; it happens by participation. We have to be willing to participate, and take those first few steps.

✤

Chapter Five

Step 3: Imagine the Worst-Case Scenario

Carin has agreed to be there tomorrow as a support for me and to tape this activity so that I might better be able to look at it reflectively and tell the story in this book. One of the reasons I'm doing this is so that I can present to you, the reader, the dynamics of how fear has played a part in my life all these years, even after 1979, when I gave up the drugs and alcohol that used to postpone my feelings.

Almost 24 years later, I'm continuing to deal with what I'd postponed for the first 36 years of my life: the fear in all of its manifestations, the self-doubt, the shame of what it has meant to me to be a human being.

I'm really afraid for anybody to see what's left after all these years. I'm also afraid of what's left. I know that Carin is supportive, but I really don't want her to see what she's married. I'm older than she is by about 19 years, and my fear is that she'll see me as an old man. That's my story, I know, certainly not hers. I don't really know what her story is. I've been too busy criticizing myself to get an update from her.

I look at people who are in their late 50s, like Harrison Ford, and I know that being 60 or 70 is not a death sentence. Clint Eastwood, when he was in his early 60s, was not a man to be dealt with lightly. I probably couldn't be the pace car in a foot race for 40-year-olds, but that's not what I'm dealing with right now.

If I don't go to the top of that pole, I'll have a fear of being seen as incompetent, less than cowardly. The other thing that could happen is that I may get to the top and stand up on that thing and suddenly have no faith in the fact that the rope is going to hold me. Then I'll have to ask questions about that.

I guess I'll have to deal with this in layers, just like peeling an onion. Every time you peel back one layer of an onion, there's more onion there, and there's more to uncover. The closer

*you get to the core, the bigger your tears because
you've been at it a long time. It's similar to the
old saying: "The closer to the gate, the fiercer the
lions." That saying really is true.*

Nothing but Stories

The third step in overcoming fear and self-doubt
is easier than it may sound. To imagine the worst-
case scenario simply means to think of the worst
thing that could possibly happen, then bring it into
consciousness and see how much of it is based in
reality.

Our worst-case scenarios often involve statements
like: "Some people will hate me," or "They'll think
I'm stupid," or "I won't survive this," or "I'll be perceived as being faulty or weak." These stories are
usually based on how we feel about ourselves, not on
how someone else feels about us. We're just external-
izing our own feelings. What usually happens when
we admit our worst fears and tell the other person
about our worst-case scenario? They usually respond
with, "I have no idea what you're talking about.
Where did you ever get that idea?" I've had that happen more times than I can count.

For the most part, our worst-case scenarios are nothing more than stories. We can prove this to ourselves by looking back at some of the most horrible things we've imagined in the past and seeing whether or not they came true. Chances are, they never manifested. I'd guess that 98 percent of the stories we make up in our heads have no validity or possibility of ever happening. The odds against them ever coming true are bigger than any odds in Las Vegas.

The Choice Is Yours

There are exceptions, of course. Sometimes our worst-case scenarios do come true, through the laws of the universe, but that usually comes from keeping them secret. If we want to make sure that our worst-case scenarios happen, all we have to do is keep them to ourselves and they will. Bring them into consciousness and they probably won't. The choice is ours. We don't have to heal. I don't think the Deity will get mad at us if we don't. I don't think we'll get punished. We'll just end up uncomfortable, because the solution is always at hand.

Sometimes our worst-case scenarios come true because they're based on physical illnesses that can't be stopped. We still have some incurable diseases to deal with. Things like pancreatic cancer and liver cancer are pretty deadly, and few people survive them. But even if our worst-case scenario was, "I'm afraid this person is going to die," and even if it's likely to come true, we still have some choices. We can choose to spend the remaining hours, days, and months being preoccupied with our fear, or we can accept the fact that this type of illness usually causes death and choose to spend quality time with the person. Rather than focusing on the disease, we can choose to spend our time talking about how much we love the person, telling them and making sure that they hear it.

Is any of that comfortable? No, because we've never been taught on a deep enough level that it's impossible for us to die. We've been taught to believe that if someone leaves, they take away something we can never have again. I think a lot of the pain that we experience around loss is the belief that happiness has to do with an outside source—whether it be a person, a pet, or a treasured possession. Maybe we've set up ways to feel this pain. Maybe we make it harder than we need to because of our own fear and self-doubt. I say "maybe" because I don't know; I just think it's worth asking ourselves the question. Do we make life harder than we need to because of our own fear and self-doubt? We each have to answer that question for ourselves. For me, I think it's probably true.

The Very Worst Case

For some of us, the ultimate worst-case scenario is that we won't survive, that we'll actually die. I believe that nothing dies; it just changes forms. When people are mourning death or the loss of someone from this earth, they often say, "Well, that's just part of the human condition." Why relegate ourselves to just having the physical experience? Why can't we have it all? As the French philosopher Pierre Teilhard de Chardin wrote, "We are not human beings having a spiritual experience, we are spiritual beings having a human experience."

All of the spiritual teachings that we've ever had in our world have told us how to deal with death, yet we continue to ignore them. When it comes time for me to die, will I go kicking and screaming into the next life? I don't know. Right now, it's not something that I spend a lot of time worrying about. I don't believe that I'm going to die. I figure that this vehicle I've been using to travel through life will eventually have to lie down, and when that happens, I think it will be like trading in a car. I'm planning to look for a Bentley next time.

Veronica's Story

This next story shows how empowering it can be to imagine and confront our worst-case scenarios.

Veronica came to one of my three-day programs during the monsoon season of 2003. As we started our first group session on that Sunday evening, she explained that she was in the process of getting a divorce. Her 12-year marriage had produced four children whom she loved deeply, but she described the first 10 years of her marriage as "sleeping with the bogeyman." Her husband was verbally abusive and very degrading in all of his remarks.

Veronica said the abuse had grown gradually over a period of time. She tolerated it in the beginning, blaming it on her husband's upbringing in an extremely rigid, male-dominated Midwestern farming family. After the first two years or so, she began to believe the things he said about her and began to feel less capable as a person and not worthwhile. But that was only one of her reasons for staying. Veronica and her husband had become quite successful as farmers, developing a considerable amount of wealth and all the trappings that came with it. She'd grown to believe that the wealth itself was a good enough reason to stay in the abusive relationship.

For a while, Veronica distracted herself by designing her own house, throwing herself into the details of how it would look both inside and out. In obsessing over the house, she was trying to deal with her internal pain by using an external route. However, when her husband threatened to harm the children, she left the marriage immediately.

As I worked with Veronica in the group setting, with her fellow participants looking on, it became obvious that one of the ways she'd dealt with this was to intellectualize, to go as far up into her head as she could, and bring a lot of rage with her. When she told us, "I'm going to raise these children by myself; I know that I can, and that's all there is to it," there was a huge amount of energy attached to her words. When I asked her to assess how much pain was at the foundation of all the anger she was repressing, she immediately retorted, "I've dealt with this! I'm ready to move on. I'm happy with my life, and I'm going to raise these children by myself." She was obviously an extremely angry woman.

I asked Veronica whether her husband had been the first male who'd ever spoken to her in a degrading manner. She lowered her eyes immediately, began to quiver, and said, "No." She admitted that she'd been treated this way by her father and older siblings, and for the most part had been seen as a second-class citizen as a female in her family system. It was no accident that Veronica and her husband had found each other. They were pulled together like a magnetic attraction to bring up those things that needed healing.

As we looked a little closer, Veronica began to see that she hadn't worked through the pain of her abusive 12-year marriage. When I asked her why she was so adamant about her statements of having worked through this and why she took such an angry stance, she admitted, "I'm so terribly afraid to feel this."

I asked her if she'd be willing to participate in the steps for overcoming fear and self-doubt. Reluctantly, she swore at the prospect, saying, "Dammit to hell, I thought I'd done this."

Quite often, we deal with these types of things in stages, especially if we try to do it without any guidance. We may acknowledge the presence of the fear or the pain, but then we intellectualize it, wrap it up in a nice package, and put it away with a modicum of relief, believing that we've dealt with it. In truth, we've only repressed it and put it away until such time as we might feel safe in taking it out again.

I suggested to Veronica that the time was now. She was out of the marriage, she no longer felt threatened by this man, and she'd walked away with a certain amount of financial independence and a belief that she could raise her children alone in a better fashion than she could with her husband.

Since she'd already acknowledged her fear and self-doubt, I asked her to take Step 2 and quantify how much fear she was feeling. When she told me it was a nine out of a possible ten, in spite of her relief at being out of the marriage, I asked her where she thought all that fear was coming from.

She replied, "I don't have any idea. I really don't have that much to fear now."

"Well," I continued, moving on to the next step, "What's the worst possible thing that could happen?"

She said, "I could repeat this relationship. After what I've just learned, it looks like I've re-created my original family in the marriage. I'm terrified that I might do it again and create danger for both myself and my kids."

I then asked her how deep she was willing to go to work with me. When she indicated that she was willing to do whatever it took, I delved a little further. I asked her how old she felt, as her fear was obviously being driven from a trauma place. When she softly answered, "Twelve years old," I asked her to close her eyes and get an internal picture of her 12-year-old self. I encouraged her to access the memory of how it felt to be a terrified little 12-year-old in a dominant family culture that hadn't valued girls as much as it valued boys. She talked about feeling so alone and desperately needing someone to understand.

As we continued to work, I helped Veronica take the wounded part of herself out of her childhood family system and bring that little girl into present-moment time, to the place in Arizona where we sat working together that day. I helped her develop a plan with this wounded part of herself by teaching her to listen closely, parent the child, create safety for her, and make a commitment to never take her into another abusive situation. By this time, Veronica had stepped out of that 12-year-old place—a wounded place from which she was certainly not capable of being a mother, a wife, or someone who had any idea of how to create safety—and had given direction of her life to a present-day, 30-year-old adult.

At the conclusion of her work and during the feedback portion of the group process, after listening to her fellow group members give their impressions of what they'd seen and heard, Veronica looked me directly in the eye and said, "I need to tell you something, Wyatt. I feel like a woman for the first time in my life." She was smiling and crying all at the same time. It was a total celebration.

I congratulated Veronica for finally acknowledging the pain, the fear, and the self-doubt that she had quantified as a nine out of a possible ten. Realizing that she'd been operating out of a truly traumatized state, she'd confronted her worst-case scenario and transcended to present-day time. She'd gotten the information she needed and had learned how to be a loving, understanding source of support to the frightened 12-year-old who lived inside. She'd completed the first four steps of overcoming fear and self-doubt, and she'd certainly earned the right to celebrate.

I worked with Veronica for two more days in the group process. She continued to celebrate her womanhood and to feel the power of what that truly meant. When she found herself triggered again as other levels of the fear or the abusive past came into play, she utilized her newfound skills, imagined the worst-case scenario, and asked herself, "What is this going to be like five, six, seven, eight days from now, or two months from now?" She'd learned how to use the five steps to bring herself back into present-moment time and create that place of safety that always exists in the here-and-now.

The Sweetness of Connection

Deciding to grow spiritually can be a lonely journey, but lately I seem to run into more and more individuals who are taking the same journey and walking through their own fear and self-doubt. The encounter with them and the subsequent connection is certainly sweet. This energetic connection is something that can't be taken away. It can't be bought or sold. It can only be given and received, and maybe that's where the living takes place. I know that when I'm in the presence of other people who are dealing with their fear and self-doubt, as I am, we have an opportunity to connect, and therein lies the sweetness.

One of the deepest connections I've felt within the past five to ten years of my life occurred in April 2002 when I had the opportunity to spend three days in New York City, presenting a workshop for the staff of a national magazine. The day I arrived, a friend of mine, a documentary filmmaker named Barry Boyle, greeted me at my hotel in Times Square and we proceeded to go to Ground Zero, the former site of the World Trade Center towers.

The trip from Times Square to the neighborhood where the towers had been was an event in and of itself. It was my first trip on a subway, and I'd heard all kinds of terrible stories over the years about the subway system. None of them turned out to be true for me. Beneath the streets of New York City, I consistently connected with people.

I was wearing a big hat, and one lady tapped me on the shoulder and said, "You might want to hold on to the support bar. I'd hate to see you get that beautiful hat knocked off." I asked her what tipped her off that I wasn't a veteran of subway travel, and this gave six or eight people an opportunity to laugh with each other. Conversations continued to occur with people I'd never met in my life, and people smiled at me as I made my way toward Ground Zero. This had been my experience in New York on two previous occasions, so maybe we get what we ask for. I was certainly in a place of being open to the people in New York City, and they responded in a most favorable way.

What occurred at the end of that subway ride was one of the largest experiences of my life, and I'll never forget it as long as I live. We came up out of the subway and took a cab to the cordoned-off viewing area that surrounded Ground Zero. The first thing I noticed was how clean the place was. It was nothing like the horrendous debris I'd seen on TV. Other than the absence of those huge towers and some construction around the area, there was no evidence that this catastrophic event had occurred. I thought to myself,

How capable and incredible of people to come in and restore some semblance of order to an area that had been so completely devastated.

The church that sits to the right of Ground Zero was spotless, and the fence around it was covered with literally hundreds of thousands of expressions of sympathy, love, and respect for those who'd lost their lives. I remember thinking that approximately 3,000 people had lost their lives that day, which in turn somehow provided hundreds of thousands of people an opportunity to connect as fellow participants on this journey on this planet.

As we walked toward the ramp that led to Ground Zero, I realized that even if I spent a week there, it would have been impossible for me to count all the cards, bouquets, ribbons, and plaques of acknowledgment. God only knows how many heartfelt notes had been written and sent. I remember feeling incredible sadness as I reached up and touched the signatures on the plywood walls that lined the ramp. I remember walking out to the edge of the barricade and the ramp and looking over into the empty space that had housed those two magnificent buildings, which in turn housed all those wonderful souls who were simply living their lives on a daily basis. I remember Barry looking at me and saying, "I've never seen a

113

sadder look on anybody's face than when you looked over the edge into where the towers were."

I remember thinking to myself in the midst of my sadness that I definitely felt a sense of connection, due to the multitude of expressions from people all over the world who, in their journey to that place, had done what they could to say, "I'm sorry this happened." I wish we could get the message that this opportunity to express something from our hearts exists on a daily basis, and that we need not wait for a tragedy as an excuse to express our feelings toward our fellow beings.

All of those souls had given those of us who were left behind an opportunity to express something from our hearts. Does that make up for their loss? Of course not. But there seemed to be some spiritual justice involved with what had happened, and was happening as I was there, and what must happen there each day for people from all over the world. It seemed as if every country on the planet had been represented there by expressions of sympathy and support.

As Barry and I stood quietly looking at the emptiness of the space, a young man and his wife came up to us. He was about 6'8", but she was in a wheelchair and couldn't see over the four-and-a-half-foot barrier that kept people from entering the site. What occurred next brought tears to my eyes. This gentle giant bent all the way down to the ground, balancing himself on one leg and easing himself back between her legs. He placed her legs around his waist, she wrapped her arms around his neck; and this big, strong man stood up with her and walked to the edge of the barricades with her on his back so that she might see Ground Zero for herself.

When I talk about the opportunity to connect and the sweetness of that, I remember that day in April 2002, and I will continue to remember it for the rest of my life.

꘠✳꘡

Step 4: Gather Information and Support, Confront the Perception, and Dissipate the Fear

Today was the big day. I showed up at the Quantum Leap and was greeted by Joe and Kevin. Both men are Miraval personnel and expert facilitators for this event, and they were ready to assist me with my climb. Carin was there to videotape and watch, so this was all set up to be a pretty good-sized deal.

Last night, I'd considered three or four scenarios that could occur. The next step was to gather information and support. I talked to Joe about what I perceived as my physical limitations. I let him know that I often defend myself against feeling varying degrees of fear by becoming sarcastic or using anger as a defense. I asked

*him and Kevin to call me on it if they saw me
doing that, and after they agreed, I proceeded to
get into the harnesses, helmet, and all the equipment necessary for climbing the 30-foot pole.*

If You Don't Know, Ask

As I've stated before, we've been so thoroughly
conditioned by the repeated messages from our culture that our responses have become automatic. I
could ask a group of 5 people or 500, "What does
our culture say about people who ask for help?" and
nearly every one of them would answer, "They're
weak."

If asking for help means we're weak, then in order
to be strong we'd have to actually know everything.
We all know that's impossible. The only way to gather
information is to ask questions, ask for suggestions,
ask for help. Once again, that word *willingness* comes
into play.

We seem to be willing to ask for help in some
areas of our lives, but not all. We'll use the information superhighways to look things up on the Inter-
net. We'll go to a doctor with questions about our
physical health, and we may even ask for a second
or third opinion in some instances. We might even

occasionally ask for help for someone else, because that keeps us externally focused. But rarely will we ask for even a first opinion about our spiritual and emotional lives.

What keeps us from asking for help? Basically, we refuse to give ourselves permission to do so. Instead, we make up our stories and imagine the worst: "People will think I'm stupid. People will think I'm weak. People will think I'm flawed." In other words, we tell ourselves that we have to be perfect in everything we do.

Intellectually, we know better than that, but down where we live, on a cellular level, we've bought into the idea that we have to be perfect. That's a child's point of view. It's a fairy-tale perception of how life "should" be. I wish to God that the word *should* had never been invented. It's a horrible word. Every time we hear it used, it's being used to criticize.

We must let go of this fairy-tale perspective, acknowledge that it's all right to be clueless, and simply ask for help when we need it.

Finding Reliable Sources

Part of the process of gathering information is figuring out who might be helpful and who might not. In trying to find out, we're probably going to ask the wrong people once in a while, but that's how we learn.

One of the things that keeps us stuck in our fear is failing to ask for help because we talk ourselves out of it. We worry, "What if nobody understands? What if they don't care enough? What if they don't have what I need?" The answer is simple: If that happens, we just need to ask somebody else.

I've probably used this story 100 times in my career. Suppose I wake up some morning with a desperate need to dance the tango. I see someone who looks like a great tango partner, so I walk over and ask, "Would you like to dance the tango?" She answers, "No, I don't dance the tango." Do I start stomping on the ground and yelling, "Oh my God! My life is over"? No! I still have the need to dance the tango, so I just keep asking. Sooner or later, someone's bound to say yes.

Gathering information means that you just keep asking until you find someone who can answer. Although you may get rejected a few times in the beginning, with more practice and experience, you'll soon get a feel for who can help and who can't, or who will and who won't. You wouldn't go up to a homeless person and ask to borrow five dollars, would you? Of course not, because you can tell just by looking that this person probably has no money. You've learned through your experience and observations, through trial and error, and as a result you've developed a certain degree of intuition. As you become more willing to step out, your intuition gets honed more and more.

At the risk of sounding sexist, I would suggest that if you're a man and you want to know more about developing your intuition, you might want to walk up to a woman and ask her. After all, in our culture, women have had permission to use their intuition forever, and they might be able to help you develop yours. You might say, "What is this intuition thing that you have? How does that work? I hear that I have it, too. I don't like to call it that because it's a woman thing, you know. I'd rather trust my gut. But whatever we call it, I'd like to learn more about it. Can you help?"

What would it mean in this culture for a man to ask a woman for help? If you're thinking, *In a patriarchal culture, it would probably be a shameful thing,* that's just a story that you've made up in your head. Stories like those are the major enemies to peace, happiness, joy, and love. They keep us isolated and afraid, and they permit our self-loathing. They're nothing more than a kind of training, a way of programming that's become obsolete. It's time to erase the computer, set up a different password, and reprogram the whole damn thing. We could call the new program THERE'S NO SHAME IN ASKING, VERSION 2.0.

When we gather information and support, we take the next giant step toward overcoming fear and self-doubt. With information in hand, we're ready to confront our fears and walk through them to present-moment time.

Starting Up the Pole

No matter what type of fear or self-doubt we must face, Step 4 involves gathering information and support to help us confront our worst-case scenario and dissipate our misperceptions. As I began my climb up that 30-foot pole, I discovered yet again the importance of this step, and how failing to utilize it can have lifelong ramifications.

To set the scene, the day I decided to conquer the pole was one of the windiest afternoons we'd had in Tucson in about six months. The wind was blowing consistently at about 25 to 35 miles an hour, and the afternoon sun was glaring straight into my eyes. On a scale of one to ten, my fear level before I began the climb danced between seven and ten-plus.

After Kevin and Joe helped me get into my harnesses and helmet and check the equipment, I began my climb. Now, when I say "pole," that's exactly what I mean. Picture a big telephone pole in the middle of nowhere. Attached to the side is an aluminum ladder that goes about ten feet up from the ground. After that, pairs of huge staples are driven in side by side. They're just large enough to use as handholds and to stand on.

As I began climbing, I felt as if my feet weighed somewhere between 30 and 50 pounds apiece. On the plus side, I quickly realized that all my worries about whether my shoulders or knees would fail were just stories I'd made up. During the entire climb, I didn't feel one twinge of pain from any of my joints. This might have been due to the adrenaline flowing through my body, but whatever the reason, I didn't feel any physical pain. None. All the pain was purely emotional.

When I reached the top of the ladder and no longer had side rails to hold on to, all of a sudden the dynamics changed. I think this is how fear travels with most people. One of my supports was gone, as is sometimes the case in life. I had to reach up and grab on to the staples, which had nothing on either side of them. Working my way up one hand at a time, one staple after another, I climbed until my feet were on the top step of the ladder. With my next two steps, I left the ladder behind, and each move became more terrifying than the last.

I realized that my breath had become labored, not from physical exertion, but from fear. Through years of working with people in the Equine Experience, I've repeatedly seen clients hold their breath when they become scared. Having seen this thousands of times proved educational for me. I knew that my body needed oxygen desperately, so I began to take a few deep breaths.

I also felt myself becoming angry, which is my normal mode of operation, as I've mentioned before—get scared, get embarrassed, get angry. With the ladder far below and nothing to support me but those large staples, I felt my legs quiver a little, and I heard myself say aloud, "I fucking hate this." That immediately gave me energy and stopped my legs from shaking, so I said it again: "I fucking hate this!"

I was conscious enough to realize the inherent value of anger. Used in its natural sense, anger can offset our fear and keep us from becoming immobilized. However, I needed to make sure that it didn't get any larger. Again, the gift of a lot of years of work and different types of teachings in therapeutic modalities allowed me to keep myself in present-moment time so that I might not get rendered unconscious emotionally and spiritually. I stopped, took a few more breaths, then continued my ascent.

The wind seemed to intensify. I doubt that it really did, but it sure as hell felt that way. I was getting encouragement from Kevin and Joe on the ground, but I was pretty much ignoring them. I can't remember much of anything they said. Carin, knowing me as well as she does, didn't volunteer any encouragement. She'd made a conscious decision to allow this to be totally my experience, so she just continued to pay attention to her videotaping task. (She wanted to record this as well as she could so that we might view it together later and see what we could glean from it.)

When my head reached the top of the pole, and the platform was just above eye level, I realized that I'd made it to the same level that I had six years ago, when I'd decided not to go all the way. All of a sudden, my fear level escalated beyond a ten. My body froze. Standing on those large staples, totally harnessed in, I felt as if the harness didn't exist. Fear had temporarily taken over my entire system. As a grown man, I'd never felt as powerless or as helpless as I did in that moment. So, once again, I went back to Step 1 for overcoming fear and self-doubt.

Acknowledging the fear, I said out loud, "I'm frozen."

Joe and Kevin encouraged me to breathe. I did so. "Just try to take one more step," they called up to me.

Shakily, I replied, "I don't think I can."

They encouraged me to be still for a moment, so I did. They asked me to step up one more step. I did. My head still hadn't cleared the platform area, because my knees were bent. Still no joint pain. Incredible. Suddenly, I knew that I had the physical strength to do this. I stood up straight. My head cleared the top of the platform. In fact, the platform was almost at chest level. I'd gone beyond what I'd done before!

Six years earlier, I'd told the group that I was working with, "This is as far as I need to go. For me, it's a great accomplishment that I even came this far." Then I pushed off and allowed the harness to catch me. I knew then and I know now that when I said those words, it was a cop-out. It was a lie. I'd talked myself into making it okay with the pure use of rationalization. I just hadn't been willing to push the envelope as far as I'd come today.

This time, I knew that I had to get on top of that pole, but I was absolutely terrified. That tiny little platform is very small once you get up there, about the diameter of a medium-sized pizza pan, and I didn't think it was possible for me to stand up on it. I was frustrated and feeling sad, and it was emotionally very painful. I was disappointed in myself. I wished that I could stand up, but I just couldn't.

All of a sudden, I said, "I'm going to try to sit down on this damn thing." I knew I had to put my body up there somehow. If I couldn't stand, I at least had to sit. That would constitute a victory for me.

Kevin and Joe called up, "Well, maybe you want to think about possibly—"

"That's it!" I yelled out, gesturing impatiently with one hand. "This is as far as I need to take this."

"Okay," they replied.

I managed to pull myself up on top of the pole, sit down, and look around. I wasn't feeling elated, victorious, or satisfied. Mostly, it was scary, and I just felt lonely.

I called down to Joe and Kevin and told them I'd had enough. I asked them to catch me because I was jumping off. Sliding one foot around behind me, I put my hands on the platform, took a step down, and let go. I fell into the safety of the harness, and they lowered me carefully down.

A Surprising Discovery

When I got to the ground, there were congratulations all around, but I could barely hear or take in any of it. I realized how lonely I was, how once again no one else's perception of what I'd done or how successful I'd been really mattered to me. I'd been alone in this respect all my life. Something needed to come from within to fill this lonely hole, and I wasn't aware of what that was.

After getting out of the harnesses, I sat down with Carin, Joe, and Kevin and began to process what had happened. Carin talked about some of the behavioral aspects of my personality that had manifested themselves on top of the pole that day. She observed that it was quite typical of me to make a definitive statement when I had my mind made up, and because of the personal power that I'm perceived to possess, no one ever questions me or pushes me to go any further. I not only set boundaries, I generally set them with a vengeance, and people rarely attempt to cross them.

Carin also thought I was quite ingenious to figure out a way to be on top of the pole without standing up on it. She said that I always figure out a way to make something work, which was kind of nice to hear, but still we hadn't arrived at the true reason why I'd climbed up the pole. That didn't happen until Joe remarked, "You know, you didn't ask us for help at any given moment."

Somewhat surprised, I said, "It didn't even occur to me." At that moment, I realized that I certainly encourage everyone else I work with to ask for help, and I ask for help to a degree—except when I get to a place like the top of that pole, a feeling of complete powerlessness and helplessness. The next words that came out of my mouth originated in a place that I'd been unaware of consciously. I said, "When I get to a place like that, and this has been true throughout my life, it's impossible for me to turn my physical body over to anyone else's suggestion."

When I made that comment, I looked at Carin and felt an immediate sense of knowing between us. She understood exactly what I meant, and tears came to my eyes. We both knew at a very deep level that this dynamic had manifested itself in my life and in our relationship, and now it all made sense. For the first time, we both understood some things about why I'd behaved as I had.

Early in my life, I'd experienced huge pain associated with having anyone suggest anything to me regarding what should happen with my body or behaviorally. That's as much as I'll say about it, because the true genesis of this pain is too personal for me to share in this book. If I were ever to meet you in a therapeutic situation and I deemed it appropriate, I would certainly share it with you. But suffice it to say that all behavior is logical. There's a reason why I haven't been open to suggestions unless I requested them myself, and it's been a hindrance to my closeness with all human beings throughout my entire life.

This is the case with a lot of people who are trauma survivors. As children, we come up with ingenious ways to protect ourselves, but those defense mechanisms later turn into emotional prisons. That had happened to me, and I suddenly became aware of the damage it had caused. All at once, I realized that all the worst-case scenarios I'd imagined were nothing more than stories I'd made up in my head. They had nothing to do with reality, and they had nothing to do with my climbing that pole.

The universe, in its infinite wisdom, had just offered me an opportunity to discover something significant.

Another Story Unfolds

As a result of what occurred at the Quantum Leap, Carin and I went into a session with my good friend Brent Baum some three days later. Brent is a trauma specialist and a gifted therapist, and we were hoping he could help us put these new observations into perspective and see how they might have impacted our life together.

Working with Brent, we came to realize that what had occurred on top of the pole was nothing more than a reenactment of something that had been played out infrequently throughout my life. Due to some emotional wounds in my early years, I'd created an existence of polarization. Let me explain what this means.

Prior to about the age of nine and a half, I don't remember being a rage-filled kid. In fact, I remember being quite sensitive and frightened for the most part, with a general anxiety about living in the world. However, something occurred at age nine and a half that set up a pattern for future behavior.

I was in my boyhood home in Georgia with my older brother and my grandmother, whom I loved dearly. My brother was teasing me, as siblings will do, but this instance must have been significant in some way, because I remember it in detail. I remember finding myself in overload emotionally, as if to say, "I can't take another minute of this!" I remember feeling a sense of desperation, and for some reason, as if I'd been put on automatic pilot, I ran into the kitchen and grabbed the biggest butcher knife we had. I went toward my brother with it and told him that if he didn't leave me alone, I would—and I remember saying this—cut his guts out. I remember him looking at me as if I'd lost my mind. He immediately stopped teasing me and walked away. When my grandmother told me to put the knife away, I threatened her as well. I was truly in a trancelike state. That behavior did not go unnoticed, and I was later punished—and rightly so. In a civilized society, it's not okay to pull a knife on your family.

That day, something clicked in my head, and it's been with me ever since. My rage-filled behavior had come up in total response to the shame, fear, embarrassment, and pain of being teased by my brother. Rage seemed to stop those unwanted emotions when they came from an external source, and I later discovered that it also seemed to stop them when they came from inside. Whenever I felt those feelings, rage allowed me to shut myself off emotionally, look at the other person, and angrily think, *Fuck you! Who needs you?* Through the emotion of rage, I could separate from others and become totally unavailable.

As Brent questioned me about how this event had manifested itself in my life, I realized for the first time that I'd been associating vulnerability with helplessness and hopelessness. Until that moment, I'd always believed that if I were helpless and hopeless, I'd be thrown away. Emotionally, that's what vulnerability meant to me. Intellectually, I know it's the furthest thing from the truth. Children, when they're vulnerable, are sometimes helpless. We grown-ups are not; we've proven that simply by growing up. I'd just never known how to be vulnerable and a grown-up at the same time before.

As a child, pulling that knife had served as a temporary solution. As an adult, using rage as a weapon became a cell block in my emotional prison. Whenever I felt threatened out of a trancelike, childhood place, the rage at any given moment would leave me standing there with a knife in my hand—not literally, because I don't really pull knives on people, but figuratively, through harsh words, angry looks, and distancing myself.

Rage kept me safe to some degree, because it prevented me from feeling shame, and it kept people away when I perceived them as being dangerous. However, it also kept me from being close to people whom I wanted to love, because I was desperately afraid that when I felt love for someone, it might translate into pain and rejection. Being caught between these two opposite extremes—rage at the one end, pain and rejection at the other—resulted in the polarization I mentioned earlier. Crazy? Yes. Logical? Absolutely.

Sitting there in Brent's office, I realized that the place I was looking for was the midpoint between those two poles. I didn't have a clear map, but I became committed to finding such a place, because I will not spend the rest of my time on this planet living that way.

As Brent, Carin, and I continued our session, I also began talking about my perception of what was expected of me in our marriage. Ever since I was a little boy, I've had the perception that my job was to be strong, have answers, and be there for others, especially for any woman with whom I was in a relationship. I truly wanted to be intimate, close, and completely vulnerable with Carin, yet for me, complete vulnerability had translated into hopelessness, helplessness, and powerlessness—in other words, a perfect place to die of shame.

As I explored these feelings, I found myself feeling very small internally, and for maybe the fourth or fifth time in my life I was able to go into a depth of sadness and pain that I've kept mostly at bay for my entire existence. I began to talk about our dog, Toby, whose cancer has recurred. I've truly grown to love this dog, who comes up to our bed in the morning and lays his muzzle on my hand. In a small voice, I said, "I don't get to grieve, I don't get to feel disappointed, I don't get to feel the pain of the potential loss of a great friend like Toby, because I believe that I have to be there for Carin." It was a deep expression of love, but it came from the place of being a helpless young boy, not an empowered grown man. It turns out that it was also just another story I'd made up, and not what Carin expected at all.

I can understand that this might sound dramatic to you, the reader, but keep in mind that part of me, even as a grown man, was still operating with the coping skills of a nine-and-a-half-year-old child who'd been afraid to deal with this particular source of fear and self-doubt. Can I see that now? Yes. The route to my awareness involved climbing to the top of that pole and putting myself in a dysfunctional, perceived helpless-hopeless place that had nothing to do with the truth. It was just a perception, and a faulty one at that. By going through the process, I finally realized that I'm neither helpless nor hopeless when I'm vulnerable.

What really amazes me is that if I'd seen this in a client, my intellectual side would have been able to work with that person and offer plenty of opportunities. Somehow, I hadn't been able to do that for myself. I remember an old saying I heard years ago, and I guess it must be true: "A physician who treats himself has a fool for a patient." Just because I've been able to work therapeutically with others doesn't mean that I didn't remain blind to some of my own unresolved stuff.

By the time we concluded the session that day,
I'd been able to release more pain than I ever would
have believed was there. If I were to ever climb up
that pole again and get to that spot of helplessness
and hopelessness, I'm going to start talking about it.
If anybody suggests something to me, I'm not going
to cut them off. I realize that this is what I've done
my whole life, and it hasn't worked very well.

Finally, I now understand what caused me to
set my boundaries with such a vengeance. I wasn't
just setting boundaries; I was absolutely drawing a
line in the dust and saying, "If you come across this,
somebody's going to end up being hurt and it won't
be me." People get that message, and they back off
from someone who looks a little bit crazy in their
eyes. That's what a scared person will do, and that's
what I'd done when I felt really helpless. I was using
the coping skills of a scared nine-year-old, and they
didn't get me what I wanted, but now I have a new
awareness.

At the end of our session in Brent's office, both
Carin and Brent talked about how much lighter my
face looked and how unburdened I appeared to be.
It certainly felt that way to me. It was such a relief
to have taken this crucial fourth step. I'd gathered
information, confronted some lifetime misperceptions, and finally walked through the fear that had

held me back for so long. In allowing myself to be vulnerable to another human being, I'd discovered once again the sweetness of connection and the joy that is every individual's birthright.

Cliff's Story

I don't want to end this chapter on such a serious note, so this seems like the perfect place for the following story. It illustrates the power of gathering information.

Before I begin, I guess I'd better insert a brief disclaimer. I grew up in the southeastern United States, and one of the things that's really prevalent there are stories about taboo subjects like bodily functions. They're seen as being really funny, probably because telling them brings relief from some pretty repressive cultural beliefs. In my 60 years on this earth, I haven't lost my enjoyment for these kinds of stories. When my friend Cliff told me this one, I lost my breath halfway through from laughing so hard. It's a true story, and I just had to include it in this book. I hope it doesn't offend anyone.

It seems that Cliff had gone to downtown Tucson with his dog in his truck. If you travel on these streets a lot, you'll see that quite often—a man with his dog or dogs in a truck. Sadly, because of our high temperatures, there have been repeated cases of dogs suffocating in the heat of the spring, summer, and fall, so the city of Tucson passed an ordinance making it illegal to leave an animal in a parked vehicle, regardless of the time of year.

On this particular day, the dog ordinance became significant to Cliff. He and his dog were traveling in midtown Tucson, and they got stuck in traffic. Being pressed for time, Cliff became increasingly frustrated and began to feel a modicum of anxiety. For most people, this wouldn't be a big deal, but Cliff has suffered from an anxiety disorder for a great deal of his life. When he experiences the onset of an anxiety attack, usually what happens to him is that nature calls and he develops sudden gastrointestinal distress. In other words, Cliff was stuck on the streets of downtown Tucson with an immediate urge to have a bowel movement.

Remembering the dog ordinance, his anxiety only grew. He thought to himself, *I can't park the truck and run into a service station or any other establishment and ask to use the restroom, because it would cost me $750 to $1,000 if I left my dog in the truck!*

Weighing the alternatives in his mind, Cliff knew he had an immediate dilemma. *I just got this truck. If I poop in it, I'm going to ruin it. I can't jump out and park on the side of road because I'm in a residential neighborhood and there isn't enough vegetation in the desert to hide me. I'm in deep trouble!*

At that point in time, Cliff remembered my five steps for overcoming fear and self-doubt. Trying to be calm, he quickly ran through the first three steps. He asked himself, *Am I afraid? Of course I am! I'm having an anxiety attack. On a scale of 1 to 10, how much fear am I feeling? It's a 10 or 11. What's the worst thing that can happen? I can shit in my pants and ruin my truck!*

Then he remembered Step 4: Gather information so you can avoid the worst-case scenario. He suddenly remembered that he not only had the dog in the truck, he also had some disposable bags for cleaning up doggie litter when he took the dog to the park. He thought to himself, *My windows are tinted. I could jump in the back and use a doggie bag!*

As soon as Cliff had information, his anxiety subsided. He knew he had choices, which meant the fear was not in charge of what would happen. His sense of urgency diminished, giving him immediate relief from the need to have a bowel movement in his truck. Because the fear dissipated, so did his need. He was able to make it home to the appropriate facilities (although he did say that he ran without stopping from his truck to the bathroom). He completed his mission and was certainly able to use Step 5: *Celebrate!*

Hurray for Cliff! His truck was intact, so was his laundry, and so was his fear quotient. He used the five steps for overcoming fear and self-doubt in an everyday circumstance that I'm sure many of us can identify with. He also showed that gathering information doesn't always mean talking to someone else. Sometimes the resources we need are right inside of us.

≈✳≈

Chapter Seven

Step 5: Celebrate!

Taking the Quantum Leap was like peeling an onion. As I pulled back one layer of fear and self-doubt, additional layers were revealed—new opportunities to heal old wounds. The process of climbing that 30-foot pole led to other places where I'd been afraid because they were all interconnected. That doesn't mean I've cleared up all of my fears for the rest of my life. I just handled one particular kind in that particular moment. I also have a fear of the ocean, which wasn't cured by this experience. If I wanted to overcome it, I'd have to get in the water and use the five steps to deal with that specific fear. If I had a fear of abandonment, I'd have to get into a relationship and use the five steps from within that particular dynamic. If I had a fear of boots, I couldn't overcome it by going barefoot. I'd have to put on some boots and utilize the steps. The five steps are specific tools for handling whatever is going on at a particular moment in time.

Let's try another analogy. Aspirin is good for a lot of different ailments, but we'd have to use a different dosage and a different schedule for a headache than we would for arthritis or to prevent a heart attack. Now, the aspirin is the same drug in each of those three cases, but in different situations it produces different results. The five steps operate under the same principle. They're five tools for one horrible thing (fear and self-doubt) that manifests itself in a myriad of ways.

We start out on a journey, working toward a specific destination—to climb a pole, get over a fear of the sea, or whatever the case may be. If we are to awaken from the sleep of the physical life into the spiritual, which is the journey that we're truly taking, I think we have to understand that all of our hoped-for results turn out to be opportunities. What if everything is bottomless? What if everything is infinite? What if all we have to do is be willing to take that first step and see where it

*leads, then take the opportunities that arise from
that place? The end result is a celebration that
makes the whole process worthwhile.*

The Ultimate Destination

Once we've completed the first four steps, we
arrive at a place of knowing that there's nothing
wrong with us and there wasn't that much to be
afraid of in the first place. That's when the smile
automatically happens. It's time to celebrate and to
consciously claim this place as our own.

The right to celebrate isn't something that
dropped on us out of the sky. We didn't get lucky
and win a prize. We've earned the right to celebrate,
because we've done what we didn't believe we could.
We've corrected a misperception that made us believe
we were faulty and that the world was an unsafe
place. All of a sudden we know that's not true. We're
not faulty, and we are safe. It's time to celebrate!

How long will we be able to stay in that place?
Sometimes it may be as brief as five to ten seconds,
but it can feel like an eternity, and it's enough time
to integrate the possibility of it happening again. The
one thing I know about the human spirit is that if
we prove something to it, it will reach for that thing

time and time again. All we need is the willingness to confront the fear and self-doubt. The first four steps lead to the fifth, which leads to freedom. And that's what this is really all about. The only experience we're looking for is freedom.

If there weren't results along the way, I wouldn't expect myself or anyone else to continue the journey. One of the things that I'd like to share with you is that immediately following the Quantum Leap and the deep emotional work that took place in Brent Baum's office some three to four days later, Carin and I experienced a huge shift in the energy of our home.

As couples get closer to discovering their individual core wounds by clearing up the wounds of the past, oftentimes the energy intensifies. I heard many years ago, "The closer to the gates, the fiercer the lions." As we traverse the spiritual landscape, I don't doubt this at all. It certainly has proven to be true in my journey and in the journeys of those I've been privileged to witness.

As I previously related, I'd become extremely defensive, was easily triggered at any given moment, and would go into a trauma-triggered place where I had absolutely no skills as a husband, a partner, or even a friend. I could do this by raising my voice, walking away, dissociating, or simply going cold inside. I'd developed all of those skills over the years as a way to isolate myself and keep from experiencing what I believed to be my worst-case scenario, which was to die from whatever I was afraid of. Suddenly, all of that was gone.

The proof that these types of therapeutic interventions work is that they're evidenced by marked behavioral changes. Since that day in Brent's office, I haven't felt anywhere near the amount of tension I experienced before, so I haven't been acting like some tomcat with a gland condition, spraying the room to keep myself safe. Progress is being made. I know that I'm heading toward the middle ground that I seek, and I've seen it happen to many others as well.

DB's Story

One of the common misperceptions that I'm repeatedly confronted with, both in my practice and in my personal life, is that when we're walking through our particular fears and manifestations of self-doubt, they're unique to us. We're convinced that we're alone. We're sure that these kinds of things never, ever happen to anyone else. I recently, probably for the 500th time, was reminded of just how much company I have on my particular journey.

A close friend of mine from California, after hearing about my experience at the Quantum Leap, said that he wanted to come to Miraval for a few days and attempt the climb himself, as his fear of heights was similar to mine. It turns out that he had many fears and wounds that were similar to mine.

Early in his life, this man whom we'll call DB lost both of his parents within a short time. His father died when DB was 11 years old, and three years later his mother died of breast cancer. DB and his brother were left in the care of relatives who were kind enough to raise them, but conditions were attached: After age 18, the brothers were either to go to college or they'd have to leave their relatives' home. They both elected to leave.

DB met, fell in love with, and married a woman who became the mother of his only child, a developmentally challenged daughter. After a number of years together, his wife developed breast cancer and subsequently died. DB was at her side throughout the entire ordeal, hearing her scream in agony but unable to do anything other than watch.

After his wife's death, DB was unable to experience any kind of lasting relationship. He generally chose unavailable women who were very different from him and unable to be in his life along with his daughter. During his weekend of work at Miraval, we discovered that he'd done this over a period of time, at a deeper level than he'd acknowledged before. Unconsciously, DB believed that if he allowed himself to get involved with someone and to love her, she would leave him. Sound familiar?

I've said before that all behavior is logical. As we looked back at DB's life, it was easy to see why he'd developed a belief system that said, "Everyone I love always leaves." He blamed himself for his father's death, his mother's death, and the death of his wife. He believed that if he'd done something different, they would have lived. He'd experienced these traumas as a child, without the tools for dealing with them, and hadn't allowed himself to go there since.

At age 48, DB brought all this history with him as he attempted to make the Quantum Leap. He'd asked me to facilitate it for him, and since I'd been up the pole a couple of times and had experience facilitating these types of experiences, I was more than honored to be at his side.

On the ground that day as he was being prepped for the climb, DB vocalized his fears both internally and aloud. He said things like, "I hate this. I hate this. I hate being afraid like this. I can't stand it. I don't want to do this. I've got to do this." I asked him to quantify the fear, and he identified it as being a level nine or ten. His worst-case scenario was that he'd get to a point where he wouldn't know what to do and feel powerless and helpless, just as I had. He'd heard me talk about not asking for help and was committed to avoiding the same mistake. He'd worked out in his head what needed to happen once he got to the top, yet when it finally happened, he was unprepared.

As DB stepped off of the ladder and onto the staples, he found himself feeling agitated and frightened. He was only two steps away from the top—almost exactly at the same point that I became stuck on the pole—when he froze and remarked, "I'm stuck."

I called up to him, "Do you remember your worst-case scenario?"

Rather than ask for help in that moment (which I hadn't done either), he answered, "It's happened. I don't know what to do."

I suggested that he be still for a moment and determine what type of help he would need.

He asked, "Is there another set of staples above my feet?"

"Yes," I replied.

Intuitively, DB had gone from "I don't know what to do" to taking the next step. He placed first one foot, then the other on the next pair of staples, and his knees were level with the platform. He'd already gone farther than I had in his journey.

He then asked for help by saying, "Would you give me tension on the security rope and help steady me as I try to take the next step?"

As he tried to step onto the platform, he lost his balance and fell. The harness caught him, but he skinned his shin pretty badly as he stepped up. We asked if he needed help with that.

"No, it's not bad at all," he said. Then he added, "This is where I usually stop. I experience a little bit of pain and I freeze. I get afraid and go no farther. This is what I do in my life and in my relationships."

DB had come to his worst-case scenario, known intuitively what to do, and decided to try something different from what he'd done for the past 35 or 40 years. On his third attempt, he stood upright on the pole. As he gazed out at the view, I suggested that maybe he needed to release the souls of his mother, father, and wife into the Santa Catalina Mountains that he saw in the distance.

At the top of his lungs he yelled, "I set you all free to go live in the mountains or any other place that you choose." Then, launching himself off the pole toward the mountains, he yelled "Freedom! Freedom!" as loudly as he could, and was caught in the harness for a safe descent.

After we lowered DB to the ground and sat down to talk about his climb, we realized that he'd achieved at the top of the pole what I later achieved in review-ing my experience. Using the five steps to break through our fear and self-doubt, we'd each taken a different route to the same place of surrender and self-awareness.

I've spoken with DB since, and he recently told me an interesting story. He was on the road, covering a convention, when a woman walked past the booth where he was working. He turned to the person with him and said, "That's the kind of woman I should be with."

I asked him, "What was remarkable about that?"

"She wasn't the usual person I'd choose," he answered. "She looked like someone who'd probably been through the fire like myself and who might be someone I could relate to and feel safe with."

This was totally different for him. In the past, he'd always chosen women who weren't safe for him. This time, as a result of his work, he intuitively knew that this person had a modicum of safety about her.

Walking over to her, he introduced himself, saying, "I know this sounds like a line, but it isn't, because I've never used it before."

They both laughed.

She then produced a book from her purse and said, "This book was given to me. This is the only copy I have, and it's very important to me. When I saw you, I felt an immediate urge to share it with you, so I'm giving it to you now."

DB went on to say that in the week after that encounter, they maintained communication via e-mail and telephone (since she lives in Florida and he lives in California). He added that the conversations with her have been some of the best he's ever had.

As you can see, DB and I are two souls who've had similar experiences. Although we've faced losses that manifested themselves differently, our spirits had defended themselves similarly, and we both found a sense of release and freedom in the same Quantum Leap activity. I'm repeatedly reminded each time I take a step, or witness someone else taking their particular steps, that our journeys are both unique and similar in their nature. We're all about to "get it," and if we're willing to share our "getting it" with each other, the journey is certainly sweeter.

One Story Ends, Another Begins

Today, I feel more free from a lifetime of fear and self-doubt than I've felt in my entire life. I'd been trying to untangle this mess and put this puzzle together forever. Will there be more fear and self-doubt, more challenges to conquer, more things to learn? Absolutely. As is the case with most of my journeys, climbing the 30-foot pole at the Quantum Leap and completing that task was nothing more than a beginning.

I remember watching one of my favorite movies, *The Dark Crystal*. In that film, a character named Aughra is describing the conjunction of the planets that will mark the end of the world. When the three suns are in conjunction, she explains, it will represent the end and also the beginning. "End, begin, all the same," she says.

The same is true for us, I think. Most of my life, I've hoped for a solution, a truly final solution. What I've found are beginnings, beginnings, and more beginnings. This experience was no different.

When I began writing this book, my intent was to climb up a 30-foot pole and document what happened as I faced one of my greatest fears. In the process, because I was open and willing to examine whatever came up, I discovered a whole family of interrelated fears and doubts, and was able to handle them one by one, using the five steps.

I didn't think I could get to the top of the pole. I didn't think I could become vulnerable in a relationship without being seen as helpless and hopeless. I didn't think I could be completely honest without being abandoned. And, for a short period of time, when I was completely at a loss for words, I didn't think I could write this book.

Well, I not only wrote this book, but I'm not ashamed of it. By walking through the fear and self-doubt, I corrected a belief system—a misperception—and came out celebrating on the other side. Will miracles never cease? Probably not. How about you and I participate in them? It has been my experience that miracle workers begin from believing that they don't know what to do, and then they move through their fear.

⊣✳⊢

ACKNOWLEDGMENTS

When thinking about the people to whom I would express my gratitude for making this book possible, where I would start was certainly a no-brainer. I start with you, the reader. Without all of you who were kind enough to open up your checkbooks, your hearts, and your curiosity to an unknown writer, I wouldn't be writing this second book. So, to all of you who took the time to buy, read, and recommend *It's Not about the Horse*, I thank you from the bottom of my heart.

To Cheryl Richardson, I would not have had my initial book deal if not for your generosity, encouragement, and the kindness of your spirit. My association with you has been rich, rewarding, and filled with gratitude and laughter. In a million years, I couldn't begin to express with words how much I appreciate you. I thank you so much for introducing me to my publisher, Hay House, Inc.; for taking time to encourage me; and for always having your phone lines open to me when I got stuck and didn't think I could do this. I truly appreciate your encouragement and mostly your friendship. It's been a joy working with you, and I look forward to many more days and nights of working in conjunction with you and the people who are kind enough to visit with us in our workshops.

I am so deeply grateful for the staff at Hay House, Inc. I thank you. You've been nothing but kind, supportive, and generous with me. Reid Tracy, you're one of a kind, and I hope you know that. I'm sure that the people who know you are certainly aware of it. Thank you so much for believing in me and my work, and for giving me the opportunity to express myself to an audience this large. Danny Levin, thanks for your friendship, your support, your encouragement, your constructive criticism at times, your laughter, and your heart. You're a good man and I appreciate you. Gail Fink, my freelance editor, thank you so much for your expertise and your particular gifts in helping to put this book together. I appreciate it.

To Sue Adkins, for the hours that you've spent walking through my Southern accent and transcribing all this dictation, some of which I'm sure didn't make sense at times, thanks for your patience, your skills, and your willingness to go the extra mile with me. I'm glad you were part of this. You certainly made it much easier for me to do this work.

Thanks to Brent Baum for your friendship and your gifts of healing. I shall always treasure having known you. You've been a true gift in my life.

Dr. Gregory Koshkarian, I literally am able to thank you from the bottom of my heart, due to your fixing it and helping it to heal. Dr. T. K. Warfield and Dr. Mary Klein, I hope you both know how special you've been in enriching the lives of my family.

I really wish to give tons of thanks to an organization called Miraval Life in Balance. I'm very fortunate and blessed to be able to work at a place like Miraval, in one of the greatest places on earth, Tucson, Arizona. Thank you to all the employees, from the line staff to upper management. To my colleagues at the Purple Sage Ranch, thank you so much for your support and your friendship. Jack O'Donnell and Amy McDonald, thank you both for your encouragement and support. Thank you, Bill O'Donnell and Joseph Denucci.

I'd be remiss in not thanking the people who've been the most important in forming my career as a therapist (and anything else that I end up being labeled as a result of spending time with you), and you are *every client I ever worked with*. You were also my teachers in the process. Thank you so much for sharing your lives with me. Thank you for trusting me with your secrets and for allowing me to share in a general way the stories of your miracles with the rest of the world. They've been important for people. You may never know how much each of you has contributed to the healing of the planet simply by doing your own healing. Let me assure you that you have. What you've done not only matters to you, it matters to others, and I thank you.

Finally, I'm grateful for the blessing of living in the United States of America, where I'm allowed the freedom of expressing myself in whatever manner I see fit, with the only fear of reprisal coming from the stories I make up.

⊱✳︎⊰

ABOUT THE AUTHOR

Wyatt Webb, the author of *It's Not about the Horse* (with Cindy Pearlman) survived 15 years in the music industry as an entertainer, touring the country 30 weeks a year. Realizing he was practically killing himself due to drug and alcohol addictions, Wyatt sought help, which led him to quit the entertainment industry. He began what is now a 24-year career as a therapist.

Eventually, Wyatt became one of the most creative, unconventional, and sought-after therapists in the country. Today he's the founder and leader of the Equine Experience at Miraval Life in Balance, one of the world's premier resorts, which is located in Tucson.

If you'd like to learn more about Wyatt Webb's Equine Experience programs held throughout the year at Miraval, please call: (800) 232-3969.

❈

NOTES

NOTES

NOTES

NOTES

NOTES

NOTES

NOTES